In-Fisherman®

1 0 0 B E S T

F R E S H W A T E R

F I S H I N G T I P S

In-Fisherman®

100 BEST
FRESHWATER
FISHING TIPS

Expert Advice from North America's
Leading Authority on Sportfishing

THE EDITORS OF IN-FISHERMAN MAGAZINE

HarperPerennial
A Division of HarperCollins*Publishers*

IN-FISHERMAN 100 BEST FRESHWATER FISHING TIPS.
Copyright ©1998 by In-Fisherman, Inc.

HarperCollins books may be purchased for educational, business, or sales promotional use. For information, please write: Special Markets Department, HarperCollins Publishers, Inc., 10 East 53rd Street, New York, NY 10022.

FIRST EDITION

Library of Congress Cataloging-in-Publication Data

In-fisherman 100 best freshwater fishing tips : expert advice from North America's leading authority on sportfishing / the editors of In-fisherman magazine.
p. cm.
Articles originally published in In-fisherman magazine and its other publications.
Includes index.
ISBN 0-06-273463-6
1. Fishing. 2. Freshwater fishes. I. In-fisherman.
SH441.I54 1998   97-42087
799.1'1—dc21   CIP

98 99 00 01 ◆/HC 5 4 3 2 1

Dedication

To Al and Ron Lindner, the founders of In-Fisherman, whose entrepreneurial spirit has changed freshwater fishing by helping anglers have more fun while catching more fish.

Introduction

EVER WONDER HOW SOME ANGLERS always seem to catch fish? These anglers are always a new technique or two or a new bait or two ahead of the rest. When the hordes toss spinners and spoons, this bunch works plastics. When everyone else fishes during the day, they fish at night. When the fishing pressure is on weedbeds, they move to rocks, or look deeper, or move to open water. And when they can't move, can't escape the crowd, they use finesse techniques where standard techniques are the norm; or they modify a standard technique when finesse is the norm. A new bait, a new technique, an old standard modified. A fake here, a sleight of hand there. Understanding when to zig instead of zag is part of the process, part of what In-Fisherman is about.

Fishing is a break, a chance to get away from it all and escape the hustle and bustle of the workaday world. But most anglers also want to catch fish, and it is this part of the process that In-Fisherman has addressed for more than 25 years. We are about teaching anglers how to catch more fish. The thrill of fishing is in the pursuit, the challenge of getting to know the characteristics of each fish species, in order to make judgments about where to find them and how to catch them. Our biggest thrill, though, is in teaching you, in seeing you improve your fishing.

Which fish species? We appreciate them each and every one, from those with obvious beauty in the eyes of most beholders, like bass and bluegills and trout, to those long considered oddballs, like carp and cats and chubs. Naturally, then, this book features tips on how to catch a variety of fish—forty-seven different species in all.

In-Fisherman 100 Best Freshwater Fishing Tips are gleaned from thousands of in-depth articles featured over the years in *In-Fisherman* magazine, or in one of our other publications, *Walleye In-Sider*, *Catfish In-Sider*, *Walleye Guide*, *Catfish Guide*, or *Bass Guide*. Many tips also have been the subject of segments on our television series (In-Fisherman Specials) which play each weekend on The Nashville Network. We also offer books and videos about fishing; and our syndicated radio program airs daily on over 600 stations across the United States.

How to use this book—Each tip follows a format that includes a short introduction, capturing the essence of the event, followed by tackle recommendations to help you fish efficiently. Seasonal icons suggest the seasons during which a tip applies—spring 🌷, summer ☀️, fall 🍂, winter ❄️. And finally, a technical section addresses details about location (finding fish) and presentation (getting them to bite). Illustrations that accompany each tip result from thousands of hours of pleasant research.

Welcome to a small part of the world of In-Fisherman. For more about fishing, contact us at In-Fisherman, In-Fisherman Drive, Brainerd, Minnesota 56425-8098. Or visit us on the Internet at <www.in-fisherman.com>.

Contents

Bottom Bumping Blades For Largemouths

FOR 20 YEARS, ANGLERS HAVE BEEN catching limits of bass by burning a spinnerbait a few inches below the surface. Times have changed, however, and bass have changed. Sadly, the new breed of fish often seems burnt

Versatile 5/8- to 1-ounce spinnerbaits with tandem Colorado, Willow-leaf, and Indiana blades are used for slow rollin' and dead draggin' presentations. Substitute a single-bladed Colorado or Indiana model for the deepest slow rollin' jobs.

out on the speedy flash of a steadily retrieved spinnerbait. Instead, anglers are working spinnerbaits near or on the bottom in water 5 to 25 feet deep. Deep and slow may be one of the most effective spinnerbait presentations ever devised for largemouth in lakes, rivers, and reservoirs.

When—

Tackle— *Rod:* 6- to 7-foot medium-heavy-power casting rod. *Reel:* slow- to moderate-speed baitcasting reel. *Line:* 17- or 20-pound-test abrasion-resistant mono.

Rigging— Early practitioners of slow rollin' used 1/2- to 1-ounce spinnerbaits with a small Colorado blade and a moderate to large willow-leaf blade. Lure manufacturers have listened to the advice of their pro staffs to refine blade combinations and to offer new styles. New models, designed specifically for bottom bouncing techniques, incorporate more lead for a straighter drop and smaller blades to keep the bait deep.

Presentation— Slow roll a spinnerbait by making a long cast over a substantial stretch of bass-holding cover, then retrieving just fast enough for the bait to tick the top of the cover. As the lure contacts weeds or wood, the blades change cadence, causing a change in vibration frequency and a sudden flash. To trigger bass that may be following the lure, give your reel a quick crank to make the bait jump away from cover. Adjust retrieve speed, lure weight, and blade design to keep the spinnerbait working near cover.

To dead drag a spinnerbait, make a long cast with a heavy spinnerbait, letting it fall on a free line to the target area.

Then work the bait along the bottom with the rod tip, experimenting with movements as you would a jig, worm, or Carolina rig. When the spinnerbait reaches a drop, it flutters down and lands. Drag it up grades or over stumps, as the spinner arm deflects snags. Unlike slow rollin', the object is to maintain constant contact with the bottom. □

Slow Rollin'

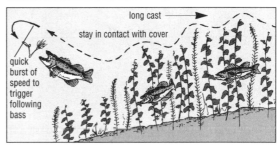

Dead Draggin'

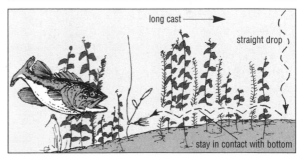

Carolina Rigging For Largemouths

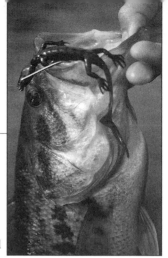

As WITH MOST FISHING TECHNIQUES, popularity spawns innovation. In many ways, Carolina rigs parallel livebait rigs for walleyes—sliding sinkers, swivels, beads, and leaders. But while walleye anglers often adjust sinker weight and color, add beads, and adjust leader length, most bass fishermen tie on a 3/4-ounce weight, a single red bead, and a 24- to 30-inch leader.

Leaders— Match your leader length to the season or type of cover you're fishing. Short, 1½- to 3-foot leaders work well during spring and winter when bass hold tight to the structure and you need a precise presentation. But for bass holding along steep ledges or suspended outside a break, as often happens in summer and fall, a longer leader shines. Leaders up to 7 feet long allow baits to drift slowly, giving bass a longer look at the bait.

Flotation— Check the flotation of your plastic baits. Most sink slowly on a standard 4/0 hook, though some may float a small hook or achieve neutral buoyancy with a large hook. To float baits higher above weed clumps, stumps, or other cover, try a floating jighead, styrofoam floats, or thicker diameter leader material.

Sinkers— Brass weights have gained enormous popularity with Carolina rig enthusiasts in recent years. Brass is less dense than lead, but clicks more sharply against rocks and beads. To maximize the clicking sounds that may help attract bass in deep clear water and shallow murky water, some anglers add a brass collar between the sinker and the bead. To minimize the flash that may spook bass, some manufacturers have dyed their brass weights black.

Rattles— Rattling lures sometimes catch more bass than non-rattling versions. Plastic and glass rattle chambers filled with shot slide into soft plastic baits. Rattles are activated when the bait hits bottom or when it's shaken. Snap-on rattles of similar design can be attached to or removed from a hook shank in seconds. Some manufacturers also offer brass weights with shot inside to produce both rattling and clicking sounds. □

Carolina Options

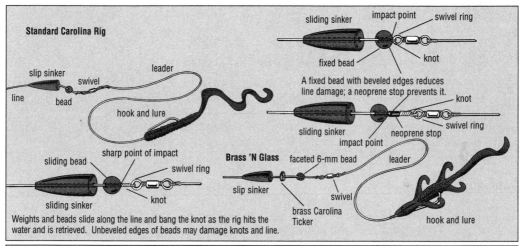

Standard Carolina Rig

sliding sinker
impact point
swivel ring
fixed bead
knot

A fixed bead with beveled edges reduces line damage; a neoprene stop prevents it.

knot
sliding sinker
neoprene stop
impact point
swivel ring

slip sinker
swivel
leader
line
bead
hook and lure

sliding bead
sharp point of impact
swivel ring
knot
sliding sinker

Brass 'N Glass
faceted 6-mm bead
leader
slip sinker
swivel
brass Carolina Ticker
hook and lure

Weights and beads slide along the line and bang the knot as the rig hits the water and is retrieved. Unbeveled edges of beads may damage knots and line.

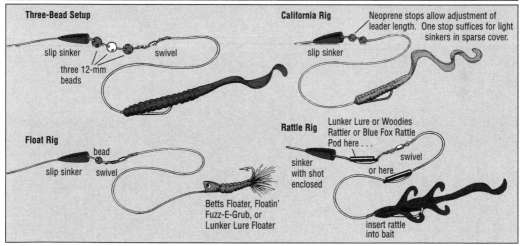

Three-Bead Setup
slip sinker
swivel
three 12-mm beads

California Rig
Neoprene stops allow adjustment of leader length. One stop suffices for light sinkers in sparse cover.
slip sinker

Float Rig
bead
slip sinker
swivel
Betts Floater, Floatin' Fuzz-E-Grub, or Lunker Lure Floater

Rattle Rig
Lunker Lure or Woodies Rattler or Blue Fox Rattle Pod here . . .
swivel
sinker with shot enclosed
or here.
insert rattle into bait

Dock Strategies For Largemouth Bass

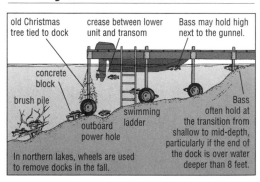

DOCKS, BOATHOUSES, AND PIERS become more important cover for largemouth bass as homes are built on lakes, reservoirs, and rivers. Shoreline development often means loss of natural cover like fallen trees, stumps, lily pad beds, and submerged weeds. Shallow-loving largemouths find steel, styrofoam, and pine board a suitable substitute. But like other popular patterns, success depends on timely tactics, attention to detail, and appropriate tackle.

Choosing Docks

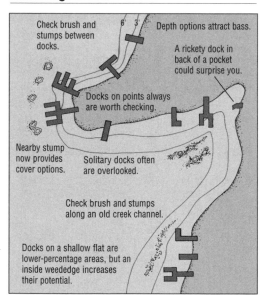

Check brush and stumps between docks.

6' 3' Depth options attract bass.

A rickety dock in back of a pocket could surprise you.

Docks on points always are worth checking.

Nearby stump now provides cover options.

Solitary docks often are overlooked.

Check brush and stumps along an old creek channel.

Docks on a shallow flat are lower-percentage areas, but an inside weededge increases their potential.

When—Water temperatures above 40°F.

Anatomy Of A Productive Dock

old Christmas tree tied to dock

crease between lower unit and transom

Bass may hold high next to the gunnel.

concrete block

brush pile

outboard power hole

swimming ladder

Bass often hold at the transition from shallow to mid-depth, particularly if the end of the dock is over water deeper than 8 feet.

In northern lakes, wheels are used to remove docks in the fall.

Flat Crankbaits For Fat Spring Bass

R OUND-BODIED CRANKBAITS dominate the market in most areas, but a small fraternity of anglers in the Carolinas, Tennessee, Kentucky, and Virginia still favor the flat designs that preceded modern cranks. Unlike their fat-bodied cousins, the original wooden flat baits were carved from thin pieces of balsa wood, giving them a distinctly different shape. Flat baits are thinner, resembling a shad or bluegill, and produce a tight shivering wiggle—a subtle vibration—that bass in cold water often find irresistible.

When— Water temperature between 45°F and 55°F.

Tackle— *Rod:* 6- to 7-foot medium-light or medium-power spinning rod or casting rod with a medium-fast action. *Reel:* medium-capacity spinning reel. *Line:* 8- to 10-pound-test mono.

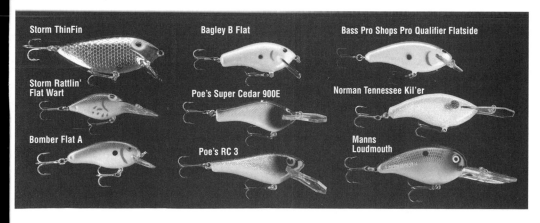

Storm ThinFin

Bagley B Flat

Bass Pro Shops Pro Qualifier Flatside

Storm Rattlin' Flat Wart

Poe's Super Cedar 900E

Norman Tennessee Kil'er

Bomber Flat A

Poe's RC 3

Manns Loudmouth

Tackle— *Tubes and prerigged worms:* 6- to 7-foot medium-power spinning rod, medium-size spinning reel, and 8- to 12-pound-test mono. *Worms and soft jerk baits:* 6½- to 7-foot medium-power spinning rod, large capacity spinning reel, and 17- to 20-pound-test mono. *Jigs:* 5½- to 6-foot medium-power pistol grip casting rod, baitcasting reel with adjustable spool brakes, and 17- to 20-pound-test mono.

Presentation— In murky water, crankbaits or spinnerbaits retrieved parallel to dock posts or walkways often draw strikes. Twitching a minnowbait or popping a topwater works fine too, on calm days when bass roam the front edges of docks. Most of the time, however, bass hold back under docks where tradition[al] casting techniques can't reach. Skip tube bai[t] and plastic worms under docks with a sidea[rm] cast, and trigger neutral bass with a slow, steady retrieve. Soft plastic jerkbaits, weight[ed] or unweighted, can also be cast far back und[er] docks for inactive largemouths. Let the bait settle to the bottom, give it a slight twitch, a[nd] repeat. Set the hook when you feel any resis[-]tance. Zipping 3/16- to 3/8-ounce jigs unde[r] docks takes more practice, but often pulls fis[h] out of brush piles and weeds that other lure[s] can't penetrate. □

Lures For Docks

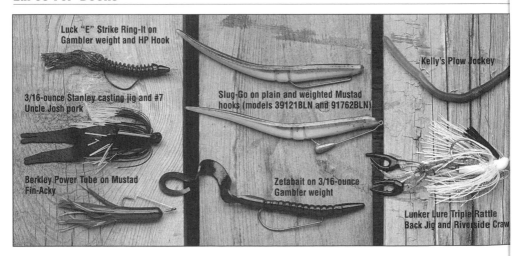

Luck "E" Strike Ring-It on Gambler weight and HP Hook

3/16-ounce Stanley casting jig and #7 Uncle Josh pork

Berkley Power Tube on Mustad Fin-Acky

Slug-Go on plain and weighted Mustad hooks (models 39121BLN and 91762BLN)

Zetabait on 3/16-ounce Gambler weight

Kelly's Plow Jockey

Lunker Lure Triple Rattle Back Jig and Riverside Craw

Rigging— Connect your line to the lure with a small split ring or round-bend snap. The short diving lip and thin body of these baits can produce an erratic circling action. Tune each bait by bending the eyelet left or right until the lure runs straight.

Presentation— Flat baits excel for fishing along sun-exposed banks in early spring, when bass often are visible in the shallows, but disappear at the first sign of trouble. Cast a shallow-running flat bait toward shallow water and retrieve it slowly and steadily. Crank too fast and the lure will spin out of control—retrieve as slowly as you can turn your reel handle, then slow down a little more.

Flat baits can also be worked effectively in heavy cover. When working through stumps and light brush, use a flat crank the same way you would use a spinnerbait, with one exception: don't pause during the retrieve. The tight wiggle and square diving lip allows these baits to deflect off snags, but because they're neutrally buoyant they tend to suspend in the cover and hang up when paused. A slow, steady crawl works best. ☐

How To Tune A Crankbait

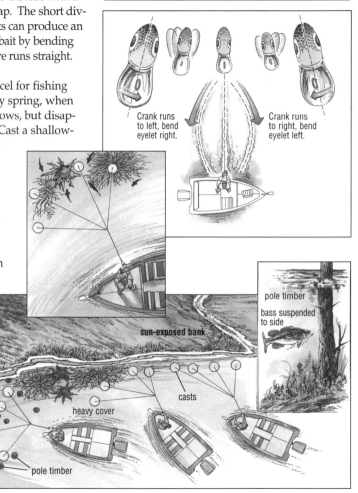

Crank runs to left, bend eyelet right.

Crank runs to right, bend eyelet left.

sun-exposed bank

pole timber

bass suspended to side

casts

heavy cover

pole timber

At Night For Largemouths

JOB SCHEDULES, RECREATIONAL BOAT traffic, and hot summer days often make night fishing for bass more enjoyable than fishing during daylight hours. But other considerations, including a shift in bass location and the subsequent aggressiveness of largemouth bass, can also make fishing at night more productive. Familiarity with cover and structure, and an understanding of bass movements and behavior after the sun goes down, are critical for nocturnal success.

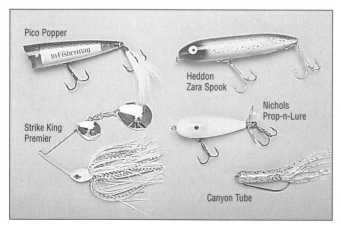

Pico Popper

In-Fisherman

Heddon
Zara Spook

Nichols
Prop-n-Lure

Strike King
Premier

Canyon Tube

When—

Tackle— *Rod:* 6- to 6½-foot medium-heavy-power casting rod. *Reel:* slow- to moderate-speed baitcasting reel. *Line:* 14- to 20-pound-test mono.

Rigging— The most productive lures send multiple sensory cues. Topwater plugs, spinnerbaits, buzzbaits, and rattlebaits are top producers during the 45 minutes before full darkness, though bass in isolated cover like fallen trees also bite jigs or worms. In murky water, chartreuse-bladed tandem spinnerbaits remain visible longest and generally outproduce metallic models.

Location— Twilight is a period of peak activity for bass and other predators. Fish move to the edge of wood cover or weeds to attack passing baitfish, and they form aggregations that move along cover edges to flush prey. After dark during summer, active largemouth bass prowl areas they rarely visit in daylight. They're less cover-oriented and often roam sparsely weeded flats in the 4- to 8-foot range. Less active bass remain in cover. Lighted docks simulate daylight by creating shade where bass may lurk all night, feeding when an opportunity arises. At dawn, they return to edges to feed, shifting into thick cover as the sun rises.

Presentation— Traditional surface plugs are top producers in open areas. Retrieve baits like the Arbogast Jitterbug and Crazy Crawler slow and steady. Retrieve prop baits steadily or with twitches. Stick baits and poppers should be retrieved slowly but erratically. If a fish strikes but misses, slowly twitch the bait in place. At rare times, bass even hit topwaters at night. In shallow to moderately deep areas (3 to 8 feet) where bass spread out, spinnerbaits usually are the best choice. Spinnerbaits pass through sparse weeds and usually don't hang up when an errant cast lands on the bank or in a lily pad bed. Around docks, tube jigs and lightly weighted Texas-rigged worms are as effective at night as during the day. ☐

Natural Lake Night Shifts

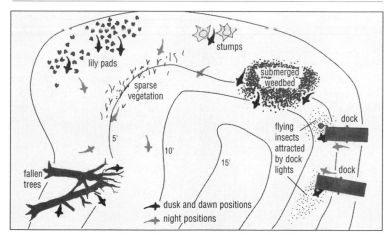

stumps

lily pads

submerged weedbed

sparse vegetation

dock

flying insects attracted by dock lights

5'

10'

15'

dock

fallen trees

➤ dusk and dawn positions
➤ night positions

Choosing The Right Jig For Largemouth Bass

MOST ANGLERS BUY JIGS FOR THE wrong reasons. Color, skirt styles, and rattles can be important, but the primary consideration in choosing a jig should be matching the design of the head to the kind of fishing you do. Prime habitat for jig fishing includes sand, rock, weeds, and wood. In each situation, a different jig design will perform best. Key design elements include head shape, weedguard, and hook design. The effectiveness of a jig depends on the combination of these aspects.

Jigs for Weeds—

No jig is as weedless as a Texas-rigged worm, but some come close. Jigheads that resemble bullet sinkers typically

Penetrator

work best in thick submerged weeds. The eye is flattened instead of turned, allowing the jig to wedge its way through vertical plant stalks. Bullet heads work best when cast—aside from flippin' or pitchin'

Scoo-TIN

heavy heads through matted weeds—because the retrieve angle approaches horizontal, so the lure is pulled nose first through the vegetation.

Bootlegger

Jigs for Sand and Gravel—
Stand-up heads work best on areas of clean bottom like sand and gravel flats. A stand-up head has a flat bottom that keeps the hook at a 10- to 50-degree angle,

keeping soft plastic or pork trailers visible to bass. Flat stand-up heads also produce a louder sound than round or bullet-shaped heads on

Triple J

gravel and rock bottoms. This kind of acoustic attraction works best in high-visibility zones like clean lips outside weededges, where bass may swim yards to take a bait, or in murky conditions where vision is limited and bass rely on sound and vibration to locate prey.

Nichols Jig

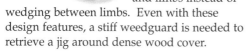

Weapon Jig

Jigs for Wood—Jigs with turned eyes resist snags better in fallen trees and brushpiles. A rounded head with weight centered in the middle often allows the jig to slide or jump up and over twigs and limbs instead of wedging between limbs. Even with these design features, a stiff weedguard is needed to retrieve a jig around dense wood cover.

Jigs for Rock—Rockpiles are jig eaters, and riprap is the jig fisherman's greatest obstacle. Most anglers switch to crankbaits, but less active fish may not strike them. To reduce

snags, use as light a jig as depth and wind conditions permit. Let it sink on a tight line, then slowly swim it. Let the jig brush the top of the rocks without falling between them. Jigs with a broad center of balance and a hook eye that rises at an angle close to 90 degrees jump out of crevices best. □

Alron Super Jig

HP Jig

Patterning Postspawn Largemouths

T HE POSTSPAWN SLUMP, SOME BLAME it on hormones, some on moon phase, some on the labors bass go through to beget more bass. Add a quick shift in fish location, increasing weedgrowth that provides new cover options, and an abundance of preyfish throughout the shallows, and it's no wonder many anglers puzzle about this phase of the fishing year. But this

period need not mean difficult fishing if you learn the subtleties of where big bass go when they abandon spawning bays, then use a meticulous presentation to get them to bite.

Slug-Go on 5/0 Gamakatsu wide-gap offset-shank hook

1/4-ounce SWAT Jig with #1 Uncle Josh rind

When—

Tackle—

Rod: 6- to 6½-foot medium-heavy-power casting rod. *Reel:* medium-capacity baitcasting reel. *Line:* 12- or 14-pound-test mono.

3/16-ounce Stanley Casting Jig with Larew Salt Craw

Zetabait Ding-A-Ling worm with 1/16-ounce weight and 3/0 Owner hook

Location— In many lakes, shallow bays are located off large embayments reaching depths of 15 feet or so. The basin tapers gradually, with slight rises and dips. Bays of this sort develop distinct weedlines that hold localized populations of bluegills, crappies, shiners, and crayfish. Huge numbers of bass may remain here for weeks, with some lingering for months after the spawn. The postspawn progression follows depth contours, with females and males that complete their parental duties moving to 4- to 6-foot flats where they hold near emerging weedbeds, sunken logs, boulders, or any other object that offers security.

Presentation— Productive spots seem obvious, but catching postspawn bass on the flats isn't easy. Logical choices like spinnerbaits or rattlebaits cover lots of water, but move too fast to take numbers of fish, or the biggest. If the water is clear, bass spook before you can get close enough to flip baits into weed clumps and pockets. Stick with slow and subtle lures like soft stickbaits and light jigs, and you'll catch bass.

Drop soft stickbaits next to clumps of weeds or into darker-looking spots. Patience is

critical. The lure's natural settling motion interspersed with modest snaps usually triggers the most bass. A 1/4- or 3/16-ounce casting jig tipped with a plastic craw or pork rind is sometimes a better option. Slowly swim the jig across the flats, dropping it by weed clumps, brushpiles, or other cover. With both baits, slower is better. □

The Postspawn Progression

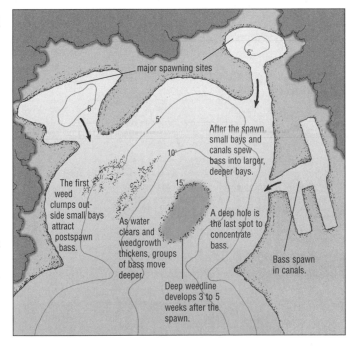

major spawning sites

After the spawn, small bays and canals spew bass into larger, deeper bays.

The first weed clumps outside small bays attract postspawn bass.

As water clears and weedgrowth thickens, groups of bass move deeper.

A deep hole is the last spot to concentrate bass.

Bass spawn in canals.

Deep weedline develops 3 to 5 weeks after the spawn.

Prerigged Worms For Largemouths

The ADVANTAGES OF PRERIGGED worms—their unique action and hooking ability—stem from the same characteristics that make these baits seem useless to Texas-rig enthusiasts. To achieve their erratic corkscrew action, prerigged worms are molded and packaged in a folded position, an abhorrence to anglers who strive to rig worms straight. The

hooks also are small—#4 or #6 in standard 6- or 7-inch models, and #8 in smaller worms. Anglers accustomed to fishing with 4/0 worm hooks often assume small hooks are incapable of hooking and holding a big fish. But the spiraling action does attract and the tiny hooks do hold; and if you're on the water without an assortment of prerigged worms, you're probably not catching as many bass as you could.

When—Water temperatures above 45°F.

Tackle— *Rod:* 6½- to 7-foot medium-power spinning rod. *Reel:* spinning reel with a long-cast spool. *Line:* 8- to 12-pound-test limp mono.

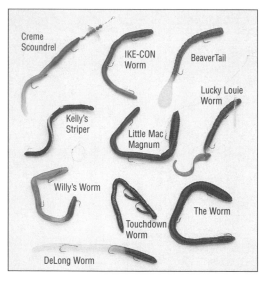

Creme Scoundrel

IKE-CON Worm

BeaverTail

Lucky Louie Worm

Kelly's Striper

Little Mac Magnum

Willy's Worm

The Worm

Touchdown Worm

DeLong Worm

Rigging—Tie a snap swivel on your main line and attach the loop at the end of the worm leader to the snap. Pinch a #3 lead shot on the main line above the swivel to improve casting distance.

Presentation—Throughout much of spring and summer, pre-rigged worms are an effective lure for searching weedy flats. Make long casts and retrieve the worm slowly and steadily. Look for pockets of sand or rock where weeds don't grow—bass hold and feed in these areas when the rest of the flat is weed-choked.

Also fish prerigged worms around weed clumps as you would a Texas-rigged worm. Bass usually position at the base of the weeds, facing open water. Cast the worm so it drops at the edge of the clump. Expect strikes as it falls or as it lies on the bottom. On sunny days, concentrate on the shady side of the weeds. Pause for a few seconds after the worm settles on the bottom. Then retrieve it slowly for ten feet to trigger curious bass that might be following the lure, before reeling in quickly and casting again. □

Weedy Flats

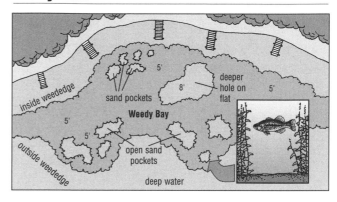

Isolated Weed Clumps

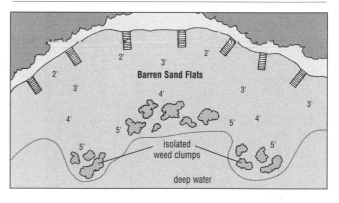

Finding The First Bass Of Spring

LARGEMOUTH BASS RETURN TO THE SHALLOWS DURING the brief transition period between the end of the cold-water season and the beginning of spring. The frigid water warms just enough to release bass from their winter sanctuaries. But these fish, seemingly afraid of their own shadows, are no easy catch.

When—

Tackle— *Rod:* 6½- to 7-foot spinning rod. *Reel:* spinning reel with a long-cast spool. *Line:* 8- or 10-pound-test limp mono.

Rigging— Baits for early season should be small and subtle. Rig a 3-inch tube bait or 4-inch plastic worm on a light-wire hook and small bullet sinker or a 1/16-ounce jighead. Keep hook points needle sharp to ensure a solid hookset with light tackle.

Lakes

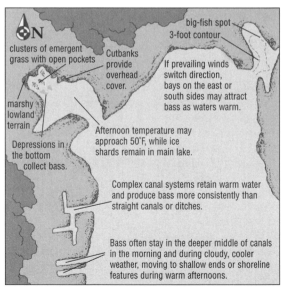

N

clusters of emergent grass with open pockets

Cutbanks provide overhead cover.

big-fish spot
3-foot contour

If prevailing winds switch direction, bays on the east or south sides may attract bass as waters warm.

marshy lowland terrain

Depressions in the bottom collect bass.

Afternoon temperature may approach 50°F, while ice shards remain in main lake.

Complex canal systems retain warm water and produce bass more consistently than straight canals or ditches.

Bass often stay in the deeper middle of canals in the morning and during cloudy, cooler weather, moving to shallow ends or shoreline features during warm afternoons.

Reservoirs

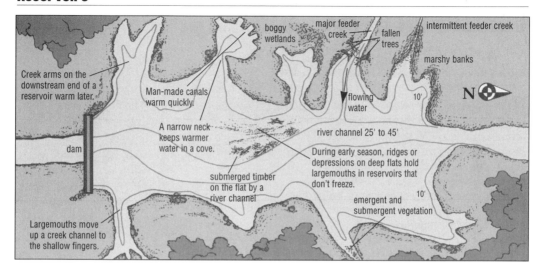

Creek arms on the downstream end of a reservoir warm later.

boggy wetlands

major feeder creek

fallen trees

intermittent feeder creek

marshy banks

Man-made canals warm quickly.

A narrow neck keeps warmer water in a cove.

dam

flowing water

10'

N

river channel 25' to 45'

During early season, ridges or depressions on deep flats hold largemouths in reservoirs that don't freeze.

submerged timber on the flat by a river channel

emergent and submergent vegetation

10'

Largemouths move up a creek channel to the shallow fingers.

Location—Bass in lakes move into backwaters as soon as the ice leaves. But not all bays are created equal. Bass often hold in less than a foot of water, though some of the water in the bay should be at least 3 feet deep to provide sanctuary from predators and changing water temperatures. Since northwest winds are prevalent during spring, bays on the northwest side of the lake tend to warm first. Bays with a broad mouth also warm quickly, but lose their warmth if shifting winds push the surface layer into the main lake. Bays separated from the lake by a narrow channel retain their warmth from day to day and often hold more bass.

Some reservoirs offer the same features that draw ice-out bass in lakes. The upstream end of an impoundment is usually shallower and subject to higher flows, so ice leaves earlier. Creek arms with little running water, especially those oriented in a northwesterly direction, also warm faster than main-reservoir areas. Bass move into the dead grass in these areas and behave much like fish in natural lakes. Fallen trees and other shoreline cover may look attractive, but in most sections of the reservoir, they lie in water too deep and cold to attract early season bass. □

Twinspins For Largemouths

THE TWINSPIN. FORGOTTEN BASS LURE. The precursor to the modern spinnerbait and forerunner of today's rubber-legged jig. The twinspin has always been ahead of its time. Today, it contends to be a potent hybrid of those two standard designs, a lure particularly good for bass in cold water. Most of the tackle industry (and most anglers) assume that in-line spinners and modern spinnerbaits have made twinspins obsolete. But veteran bass fishermen across North America depend on twinspins of varying designs to produce bass when other baits fail.

When—

Tackle— *Rod:* 6- to 7-foot medium-heavy casting rod. *Reel:* large-capacity baitcasting reel. *Line:* 12- to 17-pound-test mono.

Rigging—

One-half- to three-quarter-ounce baits are effective for scratching bluff walls in deep reservoirs, while 3/8-ounce models are

Modern Twinspin Designs.

good for working mid-depth flats in lakes. In either situation, pork frogs and eels add to the twinspin's undulating and buoyant appearance. The result is the kind of bulky package that big bass engulf, though the strike often is detectable only as extra weight on the line.

Presentation— During fall, twinspins are tough to beat. When water temperatures begin to drop and the cabbage starts to thin, bass often form tight groups among clumps of coontail growing in about 8 to 14 feet of water. Swim a twinspin through the clumps and you'll often catch the biggest bass in the group. Twinspins are most effective when water temperatures fall into the low 50°F range, and they remain effective into the low 40°F range.

In reservoirs across the Mid-South and California, during winter, trophy bass specialists use twinspins to catch lethargic bass holding tight to vertical bluff walls or to the bottom. When fishing steep ledges, hold the boat over deep water and cast toward the bank. Let the lure free fall near the wall, repeating the drop on each ledge until the lure falls deeper than bass are holding. For fish on the bottom, use an ultraslow retrieve. Let the bait rest on the bottom for several seconds before pumping it slowly forward. □

Basic Presentation

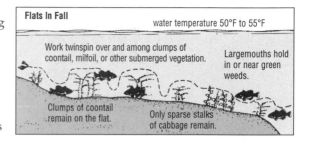

Flats In Fall — water temperature 50°F to 55°F
Work twinspin over and among clumps of coontail, milfoil, or other submerged vegetation.
Largemouths hold in or near green weeds.
Clumps of coontail remain on the flat.
Only sparse stalks of cabbage remain.

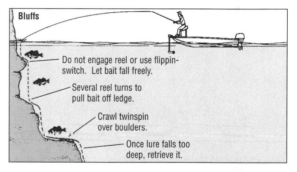

Bluffs
Do not engage reel or use flippin-switch. Let bait fall freely.
Several reel turns to pull bait off ledge.
Crawl twinspin over boulders.
Once lure falls too deep, retrieve it.

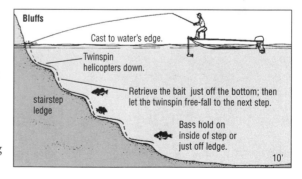

Bluffs
Cast to water's edge.
Twinspin helicopters down.
Retrieve the bait just off the bottom; then let the twinspin free-fall to the next step.
stairstep ledge
Bass hold on inside of step or just off ledge.
10'

Float 'N' Fly Smallies

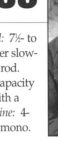

THE FLOAT 'N' FLY SYSTEM IS A SIMPLE but effective way to catch smallmouth bass. It involves lightweight hair jigs (often called flies by southern anglers) and small floats or bobbers, hence the name. When water temperatures drop below 50°F smallmouths in deep lakes and reservoirs often suspend near main-lake points and steep bluff banks. Traditional jigging lures like spoons and blade baits drop too fast to trigger a strike, but few fish can resist the seductive quivering of a fly dangled in front of their noses.

When—

Tackle— *Rod:* 7½- to 9-foot light-power slow-action spinning rod. *Reel:* medium-capacity spinning reel with a smooth drag. *Line:* 4- to 6-pound-test mono.

Rigging— Set the float 5 to 10 feet above the fly by wrapping your line a few times around the metal clip on the bottom of a plastic bobber. On sunny days, smallies often suspend in deeper water, moving within 5 or 6 feet of the surface on cloudy days. Move the float in 1- to 2-foot increments until you contact fish.

Presentation— Casting this rig is a bit like fly casting. Make an overhead cast and pause until

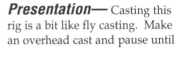

Bullet Bait Company offers Float 'N' Fly kits for clear and stained water that include two sizes of jigs and floats.

the line straightens behind you. Bring the rod forward with a smooth stroke, sending the float out ahead of the fly. Allow the fly to sink beneath the float and jiggle your rod tip so the float wobbles in place. This imparts a tantalizing motion to the fly. In moderately choppy water, leave a little slack in your line, allowing wave action to move the float. Slowly work the float back to the boat.

When a bass bites the fly, it may move up slightly, causing the bobber to lie on its side. Or it may pull the lure slowly downward, causing the float to descend smoothly like a crappie bite. Other times, the float merely jiggles. Set the hook with a long sweep. A moderate drag setting in conjunction with a long rod maintains tension and tires bass quickly. Raise your rod tip to bring the bass to the boat where you can lip or net it. □

Float 'N' Fly Fishing And Rigging Tips

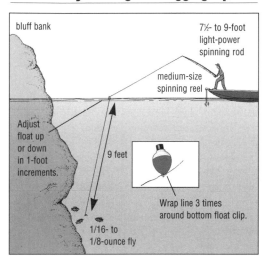

bluff bank

7½- to 9-foot light-power spinning rod

medium-size spinning reel

Adjust float up or down in 1-foot increments.

9 feet

Wrap line 3 times around bottom float clip.

1/16- to 1/8-ounce fly

Fishing The Float 'N' Fly

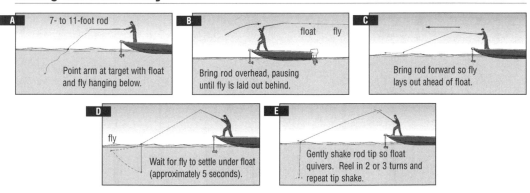

A 7- to 11-foot rod
Point arm at target with float and fly hanging below.

B float fly
Bring rod overhead, pausing until fly is laid out behind.

C
Bring rod forward so fly lays out ahead of float.

D fly
Wait for fly to settle under float (approximately 5 seconds).

E
Gently shake rod tip so float quivers. Reel in 2 or 3 turns and repeat tip shake.

Float Tactics For Stream Smallmouths

FLOATS ARE AT THEIR BEST WHEN standard presentations like crankbaits and hair jigs fail. When you know fish are in the area but can't trigger them, drift a bait downstream beneath a float. It's the most natural and subtle way to tease smallmouths into taking, and it's also efficient. With a long rod and a few floats, a bait can be drifted 50, 100, even 150 feet, combing the water for fish. Smallies that won't move 2 feet to take a lure can't resist a bait suspended in front of their noses.

Tackle—*Rod:* 7- to 10-foot fast-action medium-power spinning rod. *Reel:* medium capacity spinning reel. *Line:* 6- to 8-pound-test mono.

Rigging—For fixed floats, slide two silicone sleeves on the line—one for the top of the stem and one for the bottom. Insert the float into the sleeves. Tie a swivel to the line 6 to 12 inches below the float, then tie on a leader testing 2 pounds lighter than the main line. For slip floats, place a neoprene float stop or stop knot and bead on the line followed by the float. Add enough shot to submerge two-thirds of the body of the float. Tie on a hook or plain jighead for livebait, or a small jig for active jigging. □

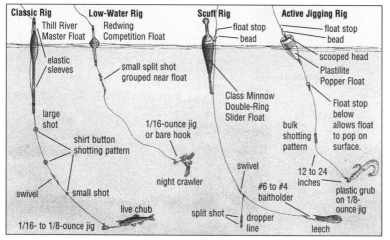

Classic Rig
- Thill River Master Float
- elastic sleeves
- large shot
- shirt button shotting pattern
- swivel
- small shot
- live chub
- 1/16- to 1/8-ounce jig

Low-Water Rig
- Redwing Competition Float
- small split shot grouped near float
- 1/16-ounce jig or bare hook
- night crawler

Scuff Rig
- float stop
- bead
- Class Minnow Double-Ring Slider Float
- bulk shotting pattern
- swivel
- #6 to #4 baitholder
- split shot
- dropper line
- leech

Active Jigging Rig
- float stop
- bead
- scooped head
- Plastilite Popper Float
- Float stop below allows float to pop on surface.
- 12 to 24 inches
- plastic grub on 1/8-ounce jig

Stream Float Presentation

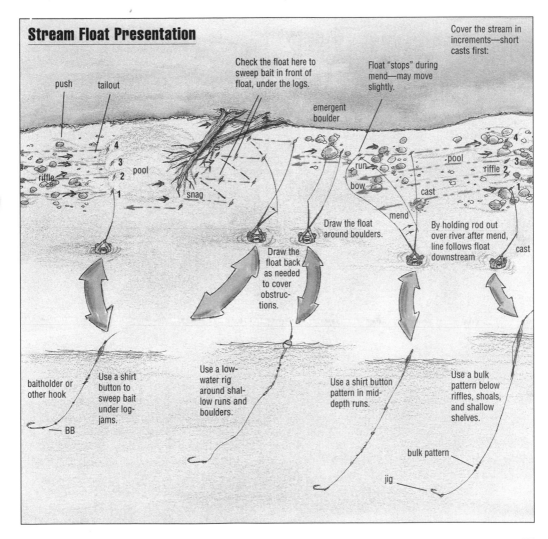

Cover the stream in increments—short casts first:

Check the float here to sweep bait in front of float, under the logs.

Float "stops" during mend—may move slightly.

push tailout

emergent boulder

pool

riffle

snag

run

bow

cast

mend

By holding rod out over river after mend, line follows float downstream

cast

Draw the float around boulders.

Draw the float back as needed to cover obstructions.

baitholder or other hook

Use a shirt button to sweep bait under log-jams.

— BB

Use a low-water rig around shallow runs and boulders.

Use a shirt button pattern in mid-depth runs.

Use a bulk pattern below riffles, shoals, and shallow shelves.

bulk pattern

jig

Hair Jigs For Smallmouths

S OFT PLASTIC BAITS IN EVERY conceivable color have displaced hair jigs in the tackle boxes of most smallmouth bass anglers. Soft plastics are widely available and catch smallmouth everywhere they swim. But well-tied hair jigs possess a solid profile, range of textures, and subtle breathing movement that plastic baits can't match. They remain one of the most versatile and effective lures for smallmouths in rivers, lakes, and reservoirs.

When—

Tackle— *Rod:* 6½- to 7½-foot medium-power fast-action spinning rod. *Reel:* medium-capacity spinning reel. *Line:* 6- to 10-pound-test mono.

Presentation— In lakes, use minnow imitating jigs on shallow flats, deep flats, or along the edge or rock bars. Cast and stop the jig just above the water, letting it drop on a fairly tight line, with the rod tip dropping to 9 o'clock. As the jig ticks bottom, lift the rod toward 11 o'clock, pause, and follow it back to bottom. Vary the speed of the retrieve and the speed of the lift, depending on the mood of the fish.

To imitate crayfish, use a brown or black pattern with a small, thin strip of pork, like one leg from an Uncle Josh U-2 pork eel. Crawl the jig across rocks and gravel. Or hop or bounce. Slowly raise the rod tip from 9 to 11 o'clock and reel in slack line as you move the tip back down to 9 o'clock. Some anglers prefer to move the rod parallel to the water, which offers less opportunity to lift the jig off the bottom. □

Basic Swimming Retrieve

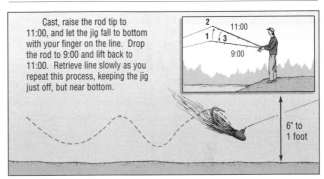

Cast, raise the rod tip to 11:00, and let the jig fall to bottom with your finger on the line. Drop the rod to 9:00 and lift back to 11:00. Retrieve line slowly as you repeat this process, keeping the jig just off, but near bottom.

6" to 1 foot

Basic Dragging Retrieve

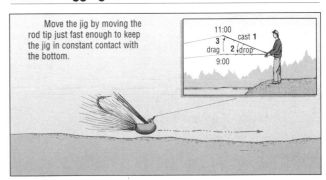

Move the jig by moving the rod tip just fast enough to keep the jig in constant contact with the bottom.

WHERE DIFFERENT HEAD STYLES PERFORM BEST (top to bottom).
Arky-style head (wood)—*Deener's Jigs & Things Fox Hair Jig*
Standup-style head (gravel and scattered rock)—*Bull Dog Hair Jig*
Football head (gravel and scattered rock)—*Ray Price Finesse Jig*
Aspirin head (broken rock or boulders)—*Bass 'N Bait Snakie Maxie*
Bullet head (swimming retrieves)—*Bert's Threadfin Shad*
Eye-in-nose bullet head (weeds)—*Andy's Penetrator*

In-Line Spinners For
Smallmouth Bass

THE BASIC DESIGN OF THE STRAIGHT-shaft or in-line spinner hasn't changed much during the past 100 years, but its productivity remains unchallenged. How does something so artificial become a target of aggression for selective, sight-feeding smallmouths? Whatever the reason, in-line spinners have helped anglers of all skill levels catch fish when other lures failed to induce a follow. They hook and hold fish exceptionally well, and it's hard to fish one wrong. But they're not magic and they don't catch smallies under all conditions. Knowing when to use them and how to maximize their action is the key to success.

When—

Tackle— *Rod:* 6½- to 7½-foot medium-light- or medium-power spinning rod. *Reel:* spinning reel with a long-cast spool. *Line:* 6- or 8-pound-test limp mono.

Spinning The Flats

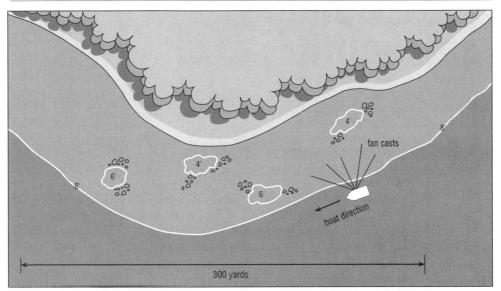

Rigging— Line twist caused by the lure spinning around instead of the blade is the spinner fisherman's worst enemy. A ball bearing snap swivel attached directly to the spinner will eliminate line twist and allow for changing lures quickly. The bell-shaped housing on the Blue Fox Vibrax spinner contains a gear arrangement designed to eliminate twist and create noise that may attract curious fish. Finally, bending the wire shaft above the spinner's blade at about a 90° angle creates a keel effect that prevents the lure from turning without altering its action.

Presentation—Spinners excel when smallmouths spread out on flats shallower than about 8 feet. They can be weighted or retrieved slower for deeper retrieves, but much of the spinner's appeal will be lost. Fish fairly quickly, moving the boat along the edge of the flat and fan cast toward visible structure and cover. Vary retrieve speed and occasionally crank fast enough to bulge the bait just below the surface. If a fish strikes but misses the lure, stop your retrieve to let the blade flutter, then rip it forward a few inches. This motion is also effective on fish that follow the lure without striking. ☐

Livebait Tactics For Smallmouths

W HEN SMALLMOUTHS ARE IN A neutral or negative feeding mood, a slow presentation produces more and bigger

fish than a rapid retrieve—even though a fast presentation covers more water. Livebait is presented slowly, but also possesses the added triggering power of natural scent, profile, and action. Live baits also can be presented more effectively in deeper water—where inactive fish are more likely found—than crankbaits and other artificials. Livebait should be an option whenever you're faced with tough conditions.

When—

Tackle—*Rod:* 6½- to 7-foot medium-power spinning rod with a moderately fast action. *Reel:* spinning reel with a long-cast spool. *Line:* 6- to 8-pound-test limp mono.

Rigging—When smallmouths are in water shallower than 10 feet, pinch on enough lead shot a foot above your hook to slowly sink the bait. For deeper water, slip a walking sinker or bell sinker on your line and tie on a #10 barrel swivel. Attach a 2- to 4-foot length of 6- or 8-pound-test monofilament leader to the other end of the swivel. Use a #2 or #4 hook for minnows, like shiners and chubs, and a #6 or #8 hook for crawlers and leeches.

Presentation—Cast smoothly to avoid tearing the bait off the hook, and let it sink to the bottom. Retrieve slack line and slowly lift the rod tip from 9 to 11 o'clock, dragging the sinker across the bottom. Pause to let the bait wiggle enticingly, reel in any slack line as you drop the rod back to 9 o'clock, and move the sinker forward again. When you feel a fish take the bait, follow it with your rod tip as you tighten the line. Then set the hook.

When searching for fish, backtroll with a slip-sinker rig along a breakline or the edge of

Sinker Weight By Depth

Depth	Recommended Sinker Weight	Distance From Boat
15' or less	1/8 or 1/4 oz.	45' to 60'
15' to 25'	1/4 or 3/8 oz.	30' to 60'
25' to 45'	3/8 to 1/2 oz.	beneath boat
beyond 45'	3/4 oz.	beneath boat

a bar. Keep your bait almost vertical and pause frequently to let it work. With an open bail and your finger pinching the line tight to your rod, you'll be able to feed line to a smallmouth that grabs the bait and moves off quickly. When you find fish, anchor and cast to cover the area. □

Slip Sinker Rigging

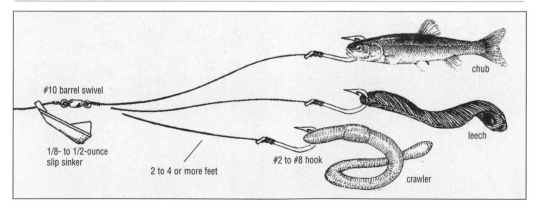

#10 barrel swivel

1/8- to 1/2-ounce slip sinker

2 to 4 or more feet

#2 to #8 hook

chub

leech

crawler

Suspending Baits For Smallmouth

FOR YEARS, TROPHY SMALLMOUTH SPECIALISTS have been crafting neutrally buoyant minnowbaits by winding pieces of wire solder around a treble hook—adding or removing metal until the bait barely floated in a tub of water. Properly weighted, these modified jerkbaits suspend and hover almost motionless when the retrieve is stopped. A presumptive prey-fish hovering in front of a bass tempts even the most lethargic fish. And the longer the bait remains in front of the fish, the better your chances of getting a strike. This presentation is particularly effective for big bass in clear lakes and reservoirs.

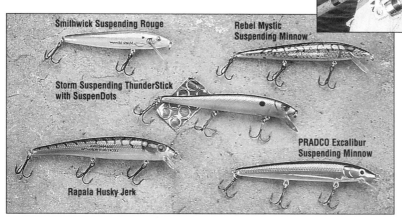

Smithwick Suspending Rouge

Rebel Mystic Suspending Minnow

Storm Suspending ThunderStick with SuspenDots

PRADCO Excalibur Suspending Minnow

Rapala Husky Jerk

When—

Tackle— *Rod:* 5½- to 6-foot light- to medium-light-power fast-action spinning rod. *Reel:* medium-capacity spinning reel. *Line:* 8- to 12-pound-test mono.

Rigging— All suspending baits are built to suspend at a certain water temperature. If a suspending bait floats in say 70°F or 80°F water, it will suspend in cooler temperatures—the increased water density holds the bait down. Storm SuspenDots and SuspenStrips are adhesive dots and strips of lead that can be attached to a lure to fine-tune buoyancy. Placing SuspenDots near the lure's balance point allows the bait to suspend horizontally, while Dots placed near the lip cause the lure to hang nose down and dive up to 10 percent deeper.

Presentation— When water temperatures fall below 50°F, it's important to work baits slowly for inactive smallmouths. Make a short sweep with your rod tip and let the lure hang motionless for 10 or 15 seconds. As water temperatures warm into the mid-50°F range, work the bait faster with longer sweeps. Jerk the bait a couple times and let it glide to a stop. Work parallel to cover, drop-offs, or weedlines, to keep the lure in the strike zone for the longest possible time. In warmer water, retrieve a nose-weighted bait quickly over shallow rock or wood cover. When the lure strikes an object, let it hang motionless for several seconds to trigger curious fish. □

Minnowbait Sweep

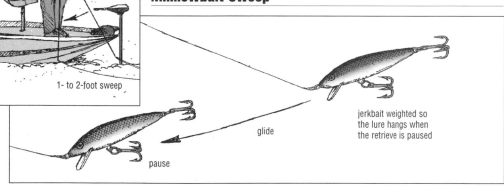

1- to 2-foot sweep

jerkbait weighted so the lure hangs when the retrieve is paused

glide

pause

Prime Time Crankin' For Smallmouths

N O MAGIC TEMPERATURE IN FISHING? Apparently, smallmouths don't know that. Top smallmouth anglers around the country point to 48°F as a key water temperature in spring. Fish are in the same areas they've been using for weeks, but suddenly they're more likely to be aggressive. Party time. Smallmouth Mardi Gras. And for the first time since fall, smallies are chasing crankbaits.

When—

Water temperatures between 42°F and 55°F.

Tackle— *Rod:* 7-foot fast-action medium-power spinning rod. *Reel:* medium-capacity spinning reel. *Line:* 8- to 10-pound-test mono.

Presentation— In natural lakes and mid-depth reservoirs, smallmouths move toward hard-bottom spawning flats at the end of the cold-water period. Shoreline lips, rock edges, and drop-offs attract and hold the largest concentrations of active fish. Particularly in natural lakes, smallmouths may also hold near docks. Early on, key docks are close to deep water. Later, almost any dock on a hard-bottom spawning flat becomes a potential draw.

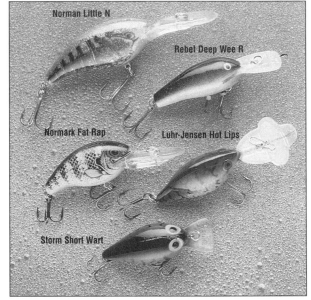

Norman Little N

Rebel Deep Wee R

Normark Fat Rap

Luhr-Jensen Hot Lips

Storm Short Wart

Water temperature is a guideline for locating fish and determining their activity level. At the end of the cold-water period, a slow and steady retrieve triggers smallmouths that won't pursue a fast moving lure. Cast out and give the reel handle a few quick turns to get the bait down to the proper depth. Retrieve at the slowest speed that will maintain that depth.

As water temperature approaches 48°F, smallmouths become increasingly active and move into shallower water. Match this aggressiveness with a faster retrieve to cover more water and catch more fish. Retrieve the bait quickly but steadily, occasionally snapping the rod tip to make the lure dart forward.

At the height of the prespawn period, it's virtually impossible to move a crankbait too fast for smallies to catch it. Reel as fast as you can while pumping the rod tip. The bait will rip forward in quick bursts and bounce erratically off the bottom and other structures. □

Water Temperature and Spring Smallmouth Patterns

Water Temperature (period)	Fish Location and Activity
32°F to 39°F (Ice-out)	Deep (20 to 45 feet in deeper lakes; 12 to 20 feet in shallower lakes) transitions from harder to softer bottom intersecting basin flats off main-lake points, bars, and related humps.
40°F to 42°F (Cold Water)	Same as above and halfway up the ends of points.
43°F to 45°F (Late Cold Water)	**The edge of flats and inside turns where deep water comes closest to shore on the same main-lake points.**
46°F to 47°F (Early Prespawn)	**A key transition period. Smallmouths make forays into shallow water, but most activity centers on inside turns and related rocks or secondary features along the primary drop-off.**
48°F to 52°F (Mid-Prespawn)	**Definite shallow movement. Beyond this point, most feeding activity is shallow. Weather permitting, activity levels soar.**
53°F to 57°F (Late Prespawn)	Activity levels remain high to about 55°F, then taper. Fish scatter shallow. Docks, rocks, and other cover produce until the urge to spawn tempers feeding responses.
58°F to 66°F (Spawn)	Nest building and egg laying. Females return quickly to deep water. Males continue to guard nests.

Topwater Sticks For Smallmouths

SMALLMOUTHS LOVE TOPWATER STICKBAITS, so much so that they often are the best bait choice no matter where you fish in North America. Of course other baits will produce better in some situations. But if you aren't carrying a basic selection of stickbaits, if you aren't considering them in most situations spring, summer, and early fall, you're probably overlooking some of the most exciting fishing in freshwater.

Bagley Tail Walker

Heddon Zara Puppy

Heddon Zara Spook

Poe's Jackpot 1400

Rebel Jumpin' Minnow

MirrOlure StickUp

When—

Tackle— *Rod:* 5- to 6-foot fast-action casting rod. *Reel:* medium-capacity baitcasting reel. *Line:* 12- to 17-pound-test mono.

Presentation—Stickbaits can be crawled slowly and subtly to trigger inactive bass by letting the lure rest 5 or more seconds between soft jerks. But because the lure flips back and forth, slow retrieves may be lengthy. Consider whether the likelihood of a bite merits the amount of time required to trigger one with a subtle retrieve.

Most of the time a faster presentation covers more water and triggers as many strikes in one-third the time. Cut pauses to a few seconds and increase the power of your wrist snaps. When fish are aggressive, use larger lures in flamboyant colors and a more aggressive retrieve to trigger some savage strikes. Snap the rod constantly and raise the rod to the 5 o'clock position between snaps. Tail-weighted stickbaits that bob strongly up and down add even more action to an aggressive presentation. □

Walking The Dog

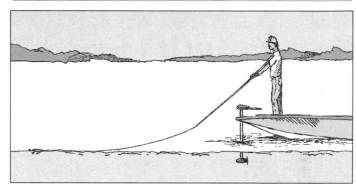

Cast the lure close to cover or over a point. Immediately engage the reel and drop the rod tip close to the water.

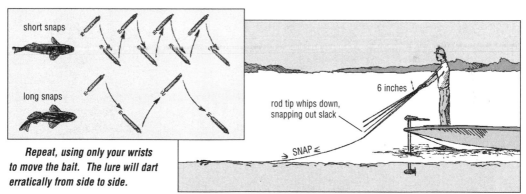

Repeat, using only your wrists to move the bait. The lure will dart erratically from side to side.

Tighten up on the line and use wrist action to snap slack from the line. Lift your wrist slightly and snap back down 6 inches, whipping the rod tip and snapping the slack from the line. After each snap, retrieve most of the slack line.

Tube Tricks For Smallmouths

T UBE BAITS HAVE EARNED A reputation with smallmouth bass anglers for producing fish during tough conditions. Tubes should top the list of soft plastic bait options just before smallmouths spawn in the spring, when they're holding tight to cover in fall, and any other time they're in shallow water. But a few minor modifications to standard tube rigs will often produce more and bigger smallies than other artificials throughout the year in lakes and reservoirs across North America.

Tube Tricks

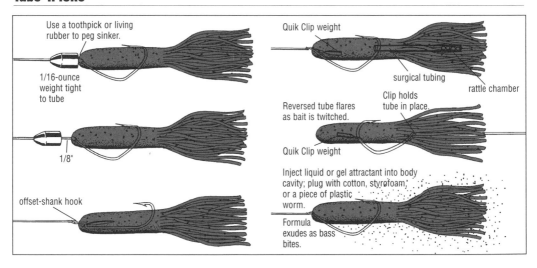

Use a toothpick or living rubber to peg sinker.

1/16-ounce weight tight to tube

1/8"

offset-shank hook

Quik Clip weight

surgical tubing

rattle chamber

Reversed tube flares as bait is twitched.

Clip holds tube in place.

Quik Clip weight

Inject liquid or gel attractant into body cavity; plug with cotton, styrofoam, or a piece of plastic worm.

Formula exudes as bass bites.

Tail-Weighted Spinnerbaits For Smallmouths

M OST SMALLMOUTH ANGLERS FISH spinnerbaits fast and shallow for aggressive fish on flats or slow-roll them through deep water for neutral and negative fish. When aggressive fish hold near deep structures, however, traditional presentations fail to trigger numbers of fish. Weighting a large spinnerbait so it can be retrieved fast and deep is the answer. This modified bait can be ripped fast to trigger active fish or allowed to fall back on a slack line to entice followers. Tail-weighted spinnerbaits are easy to create, even easier to fish, and, more importantly, they're deadly on smallmouth in summer and early fall.

Modifying Spinnerbaits For Deep Water

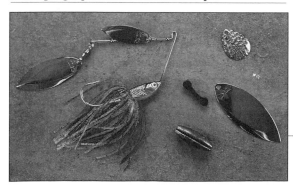

When—

Tackle— *Rod:* 6½- to 7½-foot medium-heavy-power casting rod. *Reel:* medium-capacity baitcasting reel. *Line:* 12- or 14-pound-test abrasion-resistant mono.

Using smaller willow-leaf blades and adding weight to the hook shank allows baits to swim deeper at higher retrieve speeds to trigger active fish.

When—

Tackle— *Rod:* 7-foot medium- to medium-heavy-power fast-action spinning rod. *Reel:* medium-capacity spinning reel. *Line:* 10-pound-test mono.

Rigging— Using a toothpick or Mojo pegging tool and living rubber to peg a bullet sinker creates a rig that casts and fishes like a leadhead jig. Sliding the sinker 1/8 inch away from the tube makes the lure drop straight by a target. An internal weight like the Gitzit Glider or Luck "E" Strike Quick Clip gives the tube a gliding fall, while a nose-weighted lure doesn't move as far horizontally when paused. To make a rattling tube, insert a rattle chamber into a 1/2-inch section of surgical tubing and the hook point through the other end of the tubing. For really tough smallies, rig a tube backwards using an HP Hook and a Quick Clip, or inject liquid attractant into the body cavity and plug the hole with a piece of plastic worm.

Presentation— Tube jigs are most effective in water shallower than 15 feet. Tubes can be fished deeper by adding more weight, but they fall quicker and lose the subtle action that makes them so appealing to smallmouths. When casting to docks, fallen tre or other shoreline structures, allow the jig to fal to the bottom on a semi-tight line. Watch the li where it enters the water for any sign of movement, as an active smallie often inhales the lure before it hits the water. Retrieve the lure by gently lifting it off the bottom, allowing it to fall on a tight line, then lifting it again. If fish seem reluctant to pursue the bait, a pause and jiggle routine after the drop will often trigger them. For covering rockpiles, the edges of bars, or flats, a swimming retrieve often produces more fish. Cast past your target and allow the lure to hit the bottom. Then raise and drop your rod tip as you retrieve the lure just off bottom. □

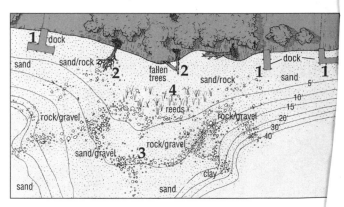

1—Use an internal weight to skip tube under docks.
2—Use a pegged sinker or jighead to hit specific targets.
3—Use an internal weight to swim a tube over rock, gravel, or sand bott
4—Add a rattle or scent in murky water or to trigger inactive bass.

Rigging—Remove the rubber insert from a 1/2- to 3/4-ounce Rubbercor sinker, and use a pliers to crimp the weight onto the hook shank of a 1/2-ounce willow-leaf spinnerbait. Lures this size often are rigged with a large willow-leaf and a small Colorado blade. Even with the extra weight, large blades often produce enough lift on a fast retrieve to keep the bait running high in the water column. Experiment with different blade sizes and styles until you find a combination that allows for a fast and deep retrieve.

Humps

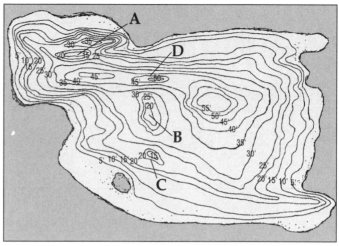

Location—Humps are key smallmouth locations in summer and fall, but not all humps are prime smallmouth habitat. On the lake illustrated here, *Hump A* is an extension of a point. Smallmouths may use this area after they spawn, but it's too small and too far from a forage-rich flat to support long-term use. *Hump B* is large, surrounded by deep water, and is covered with a mixture of rock and gravel, making it an ideal spot for small-mouth in summer and fall. *Hump C* might appear too small, but its location between *B* and the island on the large flat make it worth checking, particularly during summer. *Hump D* is probably too deep for summertime use, but it should start to produce by early fall.

Presentation—As you approach a hump or other deep structure, watch your electronics to see how fish are relating to the structure. If fish are holding to the side of the structure, make parallel casts to keep your lure in the strike zone as long as possible. If they're hold-ing on top of the structure, hold the boat downwind and cover the top with long casts. This allows your bait to reach the right depth and approach from the direction the fish are facing. Retrieve baits quickly, but not steadily. Pump your rod tip to make the bait surge for-ward, then allow it to drop back a few inches on a semi-tight line. □

Three-Way Rigs For Walleyes

T HREE-WAY RIGS ONCE WERE
considered a simplistic alternative to
more refined slip-sinker rigs. But past mis-
conceptions regarding their limited adaptabil-
ity and use have been washed away on a tide
of productivity. They catch walleyes in lakes,
rivers, and reservoirs; along structure and
across open basins; and now more than ever
before, at different depths.
Livebait, plastics, crankbaits,
floating jigheads, spinners, flutter
spoons, and combinations thereof
follow the three-way lead. Take
advantage of this versatile rigging system, or you're missing
fish.

Tackle— *Rod:* 6½- to 7½-foot
medium-heavy-power casting
rod. *Reel:* medium capacity baitcasting reel. *Line:* 8- to 12-pound-
test abrasion-resistant mono.

When—

Three-Way Variations

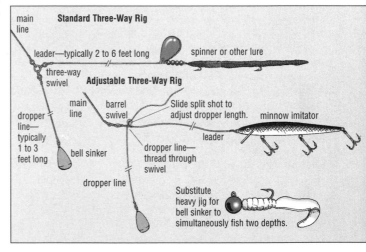

Rigging— A three-way swivel provides separate attachment points for the main line, dropper line, and leader. Varying the length of the dropper line positions the lure or bait closer to or farther from the bottom. Changing leader length positions a lure or bait farther or closer to the hardware, which to some degree affects how far off bottom a presentation runs. In general, the longer the leader, the farther an offering will droop toward bottom, unless a float is added to the leader to increase buoyancy.

Another versatile three-way rig can be constructed without a three-way swivel. Tie a standard barrel swivel between your main line and leader. Next, thread a long dropper line up through one of the loops of the swivel, and clamp a lead shot somewhere on the the dropper line opposite the sinker and swivel. The shot acts like a bobber stop. Where you set it determines the distance the swivel rides above bottom, and thus the depth the lure or bait runs. If you snag, a firm pull slides the shot off your dropper line and allows the rig to pull free of the snagged weight.

To feed more line to soft-biting fish, try a double-barreled rig. First tie a standard dropper line and weight to one loop of a barrel swivel. Next, thread your main line through the opposite loop of the swivel, then tie it to a second swivel connected to your leader. Substitute a bobber stop and bead for the second swivel, and you can easily adjust leader length as well. ☐

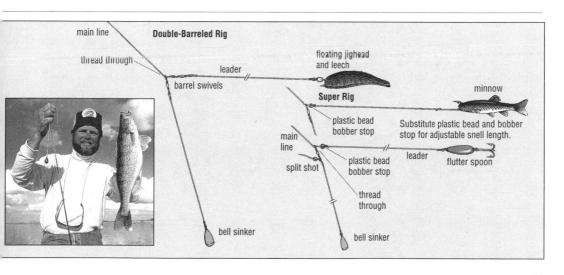

main line
Double-Barreled Rig
thread through
leader
barrel swivels

floating jighead and leech
minnow

Super Rig

plastic bead bobber stop
Substitute plastic bead and bobber stop for adjustable snell length.

main line

plastic bead bobber stop
leader
flutter spoon

split shot

thread through

bell sinker

bell sinker

Bottom Bouncers For Walleyes

Bottom bouncers are the solution to presenting livebait at a steady pace a scant few inches above snaggy bottoms, flats, or open basins. A wire feeler arm on most bouncers minimizes hang-ups while scratching upright across rocks and rubble. They also can be fished vertically on a short line, even hovered in place, so long as you avoid slack and don't let 'em topple over and snag. Different designs offer presentation options for fine-tuning livebait delivery.

When—

The Basic Bouncer Rig

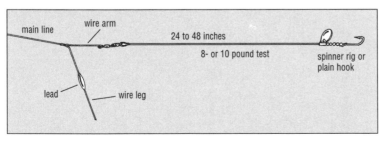

main line — wire arm — 24 to 48 inches — 8- or 10 pound test — spinner rig or plain hook

lead — wire leg

Tackle—*Rod:* 6- to 7-foot medium-power casting rod. *Reel:* medium-capacity casting reel. *Line:* 10-pound-test mono.

Rigging—Most bouncers are designed to present spinner rigs at modest speeds, though they also work well at slow speeds with livebait snells and floater snells, and at higher speeds with flutter spoons. Weight selection, therefore, depends on a combination of depth and speed. Use 1/2- to 1-ounce models for water shallower than 15 feet, 1½- to 2-ouncers for 15 to 20 feet, and 2½- to 3-ounce weights in 30- to 40-foot depths. On most bouncers, a lead weight is molded onto a bent wire shaft, with the wire protruding below the sinker to deflect snags. The other end has a snap for attaching snells or tying leaders. Tie the line to the eye at the intersection of the two wire arms.

The standard spinner rig is about 30 inches long, with a #3 or #4 Colorado blade. Switch to a larger #5 for more vibration, or to Indiana blades for less thump. Popular colors include hot orange, yellow, or chartreuse for darker water; nickel, silver, or nonfluorescent colors for clear water; and copper, gold, or neutral colors for conditions in between.

Use a two-hook harness tied with #6 hooks for night crawlers. Insert the forward hook lightly through the crawler's nose, the second partway down and into but not out of the body so the the crawler trails naturally behind the spinner. Use a single hook for sucker-hooked leeches and lip-hooked minnows. □

Hooking Bait For Bouncer Rigs

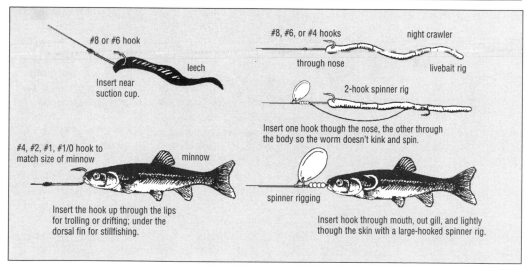

#8 or #6 hook

leech

Insert near suction cup.

#8, #6, or #4 hooks — night crawler

through nose — livebait rig

2-hook spinner rig

Insert one hook though the nose, the other through the body so the worm doesn't kink and spin.

#4, #2, #1, #1/0 hook to match size of minnow — minnow

Insert the hook up through the lips for trolling or drifting; under the dorsal fin for stillfishing.

spinner rigging

Insert hook through mouth, out gill, and lightly though the skin with a large-hooked spinner rig.

Cranking Strategies For Walleyes

LIVEBAIT IS UNBEATABLE FOR TEMPTING and teasing fussy fish into biting during tough conditions. In many situations, though, walleyes are so aggressive they don't require a slow-moving presentation. In fact, when fish are spread on flats, suspended, or roaming basins, something with a little get up and go helps to quickly eliminate unproductive water and locate fish. You can always switch to something else once you find fish. But most times, there's no need. Cranks don't just locate, they catch too.

When—

Tackle—

Rod: 6½- to 7½-foot spinning or casting rod. *Reel:* long-cast spinning reel or medium-capacity baitcasting reel. *Line:* 8- to 12-pound-test mono.

Presentation— In shallow water, slowly troll minnow imitators across flats and points on 100 feet or more of line. Use a slow, S-shape trolling pattern to probe different depths, cover areas outside the boat's path, and impart a subtle speed-up, slow-down motion to lures. Casting often is more effective on large bodies of water where big walleyes follow baitfish into the shallows at night. Select a lure that just barely nicks bottoms like rock or sand, or one that rides just above the weed tops or wood snags. Shad baits or minnow imitators generally work best. Consider weighting a minnow imitator with adhesive Storm SuspenDots to make it hover when you pause the retrieve.

In deeper water, use deep-diving crankbaits to troll the 10- to 25-foot-deep edge of classic rock or weed points, humps, and river channels. Let out enough line behind the boat so lures reach the target depth when trolled at about 1 to 1½ mph. Occasionally bump bottom to make sure lures are in the fish zone. A three-way rig with a 2-foot dropper, 3-ounce bell sinker, and 5-foot leader is an effective way to present minnow imitators at the base of deep structure. Hook a piece of night crawler on the lead treble hook of a banana bait for a different action and added scent. Troll or drift just fast enough to wobble the lure. □

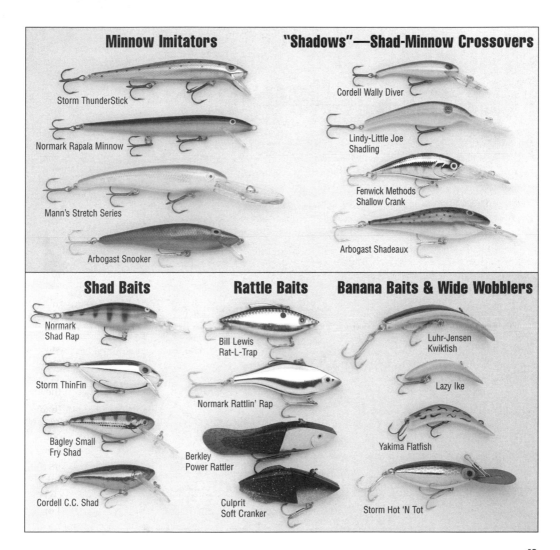

Minnow Imitators

Storm ThunderStick

Normark Rapala Minnow

Mann's Stretch Series

Arbogast Snooker

"Shadows"—Shad-Minnow Crossovers

Cordell Wally Diver

Lindy-Little Joe Shadling

Fenwick Methods Shallow Crank

Arbogast Shadeaux

Shad Baits

Normark Shad Rap

Storm ThinFin

Bagley Small Fry Shad

Cordell C.C. Shad

Rattle Baits

Bill Lewis Rat-L-Trap

Normark Rattlin' Rap

Berkley Power Rattler

Culprit Soft Cranker

Banana Baits & Wide Wobblers

Luhr-Jensen Kwikfish

Lazy Ike

Yakima Flatfish

Storm Hot 'N Tot

Jigging For Winter Walleyes

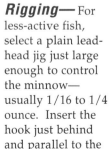

C ATCHING MORE WALLEYES THROUGH the ice is as easy as one-two-three. With three basic jig styles, you can match your offering to the activity level of the fish. From least to most aggressive, the jig types include: bare-bones leadhead jigs tipped with minnows, flash lures like the Bay De Noc Swedish Pimple and Acme Kastmaster spoons, and swimming lures like the Normark Jigging Rapala. Use these three lures and a few basic guidelines, singly or in some combination, to catch walleyes throughout the frozen-water season.

Tackle—

Rod: 28- to 36-inch medium-heavy-power ice rod with a fast action. *Reel:* spinning reel with a medium-diameter spool and a smooth drag. *Line:* 8- to 12-pound-test mono.

Rigging— For

less-active fish, select a plain leadhead jig just large enough to control the minnow— usually 1/16 to 1/4 ounce. Insert the hook just behind and parallel to the the dorsal fin of a

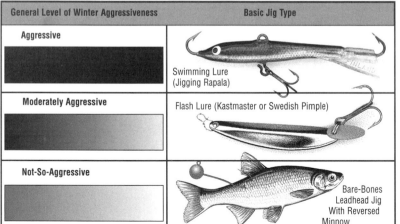

General Level of Winter Aggressiveness	Basic Jig Type
Aggressive	Swimming Lure (Jigging Rapala)
Moderately Aggressive	Flash Lure (Kastmaster or Swedish Pimple)
Not-So-Aggressive	Bare-Bones Leadhead Jig With Reversed Minnow

3- to 5-inch minnow. Swimming and flash lures should be attached to the line with a snap or split ring. Tip the treble hook with a minnow head.

Presentation— All three jig styles are presented in the same way—just add more snap and movement to aggressive lure styles to trigger active fish. Begin with the bait 3 to 9 inches off the bottom and lift the bait 1½ to 3 feet. Immediately return the rod tip to the starting position, allowing the bait to swim, flutter, or fall on a slack line. Pause several seconds before repeating, or jiggle the bait in place by subtly moving the rod tip up and down 1/16 inch. The movement, flash, and vibration of the bait attracts, while the return and pause triggers. □

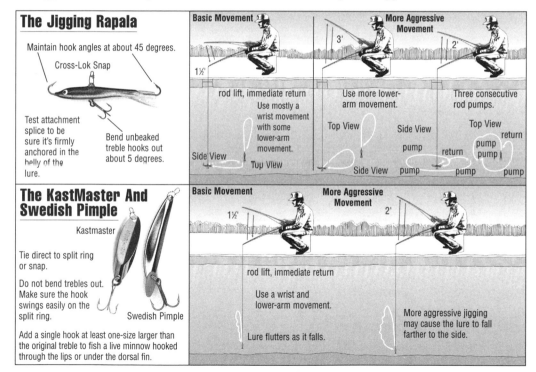

The Jigging Rapala

Maintain hook angles at about 45 degrees.

Cross-Lok Snap

Test attachment splice to be sure it's firmly anchored in the belly of the lure.

Bend unbeaked treble hooks out about 5 degrees.

Basic Movement

1½'

rod lift, immediate return
Use mostly a wrist movement with some lower-arm movement.

Side View

Top View

More Aggressive Movement

3'

Use more lower-arm movement.

Top View

Side View

2'

Three consecutive rod pumps.

Top View

return
pump
return
pump
pump

Side View
pump   pump   pump

The KastMaster And Swedish Pimple

Kastmaster

Tie direct to split ring or snap.

Do not bend trebles out. Make sure the hook swings easily on the split ring.

Swedish Pimple

Add a single hook at least one-size larger than the original treble to fish a live minnow hooked through the lips or under the dorsal fin.

Basic Movement

1½'

rod lift, immediate return

Use a wrist and lower-arm movement.

Lure flutters as it falls.

More Aggressive Movement

2'

More aggressive jigging may cause the lure to fall farther to the side.

Lighted Floats For Walleyes At Night

O N LAKES WITH HEAVY RECREATIONAL traffic and daytime fishing pressure, night fishing is one of the best ways to catch big walleyes. While there are many ways to catch walleyes in the dark—longline trolling flats with crankbaits and casting minnow imitators over the tops of reefs are both good options—drifting live-bait beneath lighted floats is one of the simplest and most effective. It blends stealth and control for fishing key spots that concentrate fish after dark. Rig gear and mark locations during daylight, and be ready for fast action when the sun sets.

Tackle— *Rod:* 6½- to 7½-foot medium-power medium-fast-action spinning rod. *Reel:* medium-capacity spinning reel. *Line:* 6- or 8-pound-test mono.

When—

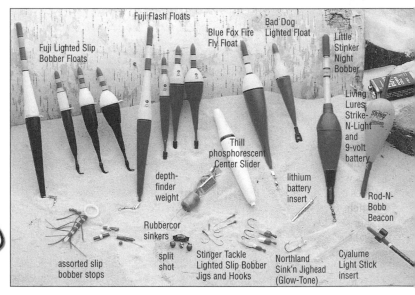

Fuji Flash Floats

Fuji Lighted Slip Bobber Floats

Blue Fox Fire Fly Float

Bad Dog Lighted Float

Little Stinker Night Bobber

Living Lures Strike-N-Light and 9-volt battery

Thill phosphorescent Center Slider

depth-finder weight

lithium battery insert

Rod-N-Bobb Beacon

Rubbercor sinkers

split shot

Stinger Tackle Lighted Slip Bobber Jigs and Hooks

Northland Sink'n Jighead (Glow-Tone)

Cyalume Light Stick insert

assorted slip bobber stops

Rigging—Lighted floats come in several versions. Most common are those with lithium battery inserts that cause a diode to glow red at the tip of the float. Some have tiny replaceable Cyalume light sticks that glow for several hours. Others are coated with phosphorescent paint that must be recharged with a flashlight or camera flash at frequent intervals. These usually are lighter and less expensive than battery-powered floats, though they seldom glow as brightly and are more difficult to see.

Fixed floats are adequate down to depths of about 5 feet. Set deeper, rigs become awkward to cast. Slip floats are more practical except in extremely shallow water. They require a sliding bobber stop to suspend bait at the selected depth. Rather than approximating the depth of the stop, attach an ice-fishing depthfinder weight to the hook and lower it to the bottom. Slide the stop up or down the line until the float is a foot or two below the surface when the depthfinder weight is on the bottom. Remove the weight and the bait will suspend just above the rocks or weeds.

Presentation—Many anglers concentrate on the tops of rock bars for walleyes at night. Bays with low-lying weed flats or the outer edges of heavy weed flats where the growth switches to a low-lying carpet of sandgrass or other short vegetation also is a key area. One ideal situation is an 8- to 12-foot carpeted flat with scattered clumps of coontail or cabbage to concentrate fish. Set float rigs to suspend bait two feet off the bottom, a foot above the weeds.

Fishing Deep Weed Carpets

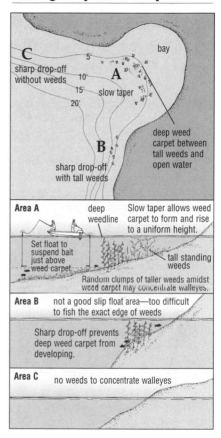

Drift the area until you contact fish, then anchor and cast. Retrieve the float with frequent pauses to allow the bait to work. □

Livebait Rigging For Walleyes

LIVEBAIT RIGS CONSIST OF HOOK, LINE, and sinker. What could be simpler? But sometimes, anything less than finesse won't do. Cold fronts send walleyes into hibernation, or at least reduce their enthusiasm for feeding. Fishing pressure makes them spooky—too many rigs dancing along the drop-off, too many of their buddies disappearing. Clear water accentuates the unnatural aspects of a poor presentation. Adjusting leader length, adding blades or beads for attraction, and using the best livebait are important factors in each situation.

When—

Tackle— *Rod:* 6- to 7-foot medium-power spinning rod. *Reel:* medium-capacity spinning reel. *Line:* 6- to 10-pound-test mono.

Weight Placement Determines Control

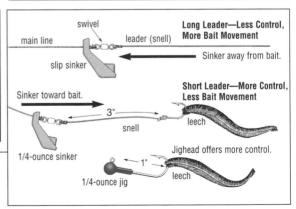

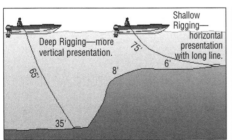

The closer the weight is to your bait, the more control you have. A minnow, worm, or leech hooked on a jig is as close as you can bring a bait to a sinker, which is what the head of a jig is.

Presentation—When searching for active fish, start with a 18- to 24-inch leader, or a longer leader and a floating jighead. Move the bait along for about 15 feet and stop. Keep your line tight to the sinker while the minnow or leech struggles in place. Wait 10 seconds for following fish to tap the bait. If nothing happens, scoot along quickly for another 15 feet and stop. This approach with a 12-inch leader works in rivers for fish holding close to the bottom.

Generally, the deeper the water the more vertically you should fish a rig. In water shallower than 6 feet, use a cast-troll presentation. Position your boat over deep water upwind from the structural element and cast toward the shallows. Troll with the same move-stop approach at an angle to the shallow portion of the bar until the bait moves into deep water. Reel in, cast again, and troll for another 80 or so feet. If you find fish, anchor and cast. □

Rigging Options

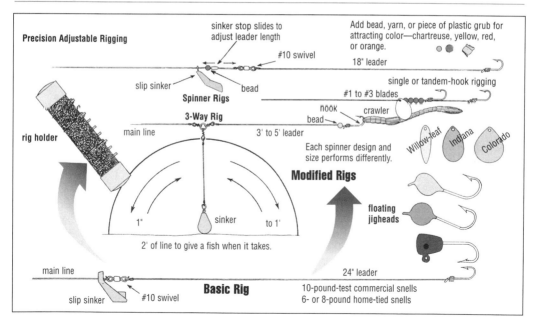

Shoreline Casting At Night For Walleyes

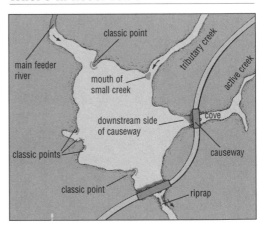

WALLEYES POSSESS A LOWLIGHT vision advantage over many forms of prey. Perch that become inactive at sunset provide easy meals during the transition period between light and dark. Yet walleyes often continue feeding into the night, savaging shiners, ciscoes, shad, or other targets of opportunity. That doesn't mean they're not cautious; sudden unnatural sounds alert them to your presence, and they shut down or flee the area. If you're relatively stealthy, however, it's possible to catch them with their guard down.

When—

Tackle— *Rod:* 6½- to 7½-foot fast-action medium-power spinning rod. *Reel:* spinning reel with a long-cast spool. *Line:* 8- to 12-pound-test mono.

Presentation— Whether you wade, fish from shore, or from a boat, shorelines are the primary starting point for checking the nocturnal potential of a fishery. On lakes, rivers, or reservoirs, anywhere current enters or passes through narrows,

crankbaits and jigs are prime methods for catching walleyes. Shallow-running crankbaits, in particular, are preferred since they're easy to carry and use—no fussing with livebait. Heavier versions cast a long distance into the darkness; lighter models are more subtle but offer a reduced range.

Where In Reservoirs

classic point

main feeder river

tributary creek

active creek

mouth of small creek

downstream side of causeway

cove

classic points

causeway

classic point

riprap

In general, minnow imitators dive only a foot or two and are ideal for skimming shallow rocks or weedtops. Use slow, steady retrieves. Particularly good are neutral buoyancy lures like Storm Suspending ThunderSticks or Normark Rapala Husky Jerks. Or make floating lures neutrally buoyant by placing adhesive Storm SuspenDots along the belly of the bait until it hangs motionless in the water. Creek mouths, piers, breakwalls, rock points, and other fish attractors are all good sites for pitching cranks.

Jigheads dressed with plastic tails back up crankbaits for a more bottom-oriented approach. Livebait generally isn't necessary; shad tails or twister tails entice strikes. Use steady retrieves to occasionally skim bottom. □

Where In Rivers

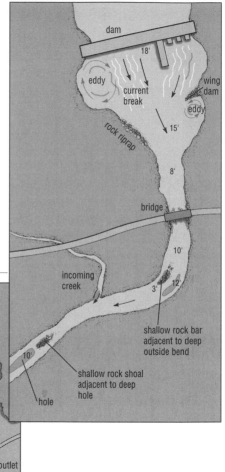

Where In Lakes

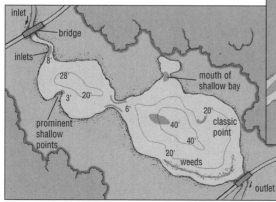

Planer Board Trolling For Walleyes

P LANER BOARD TROLLING incorporates a blend of traditional long-line trolling with precision depth coverage, eliminating vast areas of unproductive water to zero in on sections that hold fish. Planers take lines and lures out to the sides of the boat, allowing anglers to cover a wider trolling swath, simultaneously run multiple baits, and minimize spooking fish in clear or shallow water. It's particularly effective when walleyes are moving between areas. At other times, fish may be attracted to a general area by structural features like points, humps, islands, or channels, but they suspend when they're not relating to the structure itself. Any time walleyes roam the basin, down and out trolling tactics can score big.

When—

Tackle—

Rod: 7½- to 8-foot medium-power casting rod with a parabolic action. *Reel:* large-capacity baitcasting or line-counting reel with a smooth drag. *Line:* 10-pound-test monofilament or fused polyethylene line.

Rigging—In-line planers clamp onto line with one or more release clips. Run your lure behind the boat at a slow trolling speed until it reaches the desired distance, then engage the reel. Add a snap weight with a pinch-on clip 50 feet ahead of the lure for fishing deeper than the lure can run on its own. Next, clamp the planer to the line, selecting a left or right model depending on which side of the boat you want to run your line. Lower the planer into the water with the rod and disengage the reel. A slow trolling speed creates enough drag to pull line off the reel and angle the planer off to the side of the boat. Once it reaches the desired distance, engage the reel and set the rod in a rod holder.

Presentation—Strikes aren't always obvious, so watch your boards carefully. Sometimes the

planer bobs and weaves, dropping back when a big fish hits your lure. Other times, the board barely lags or rocks as a hooked fish swims along with the boat. When a fish hits, shift the engine into neutral. Take the rod out of the holder and begin slowly reeling in. Don't pump the rod. Your drag should be set light enough to slip under fairly light tension. Continue reeling until you can reach the board, then pop it off the line. Follow the same procedure with your snap weight. Then land the fish. □

Fishing High And Low

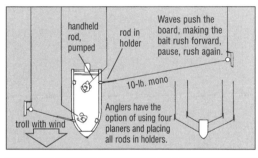

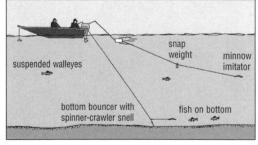

Weighting Systems

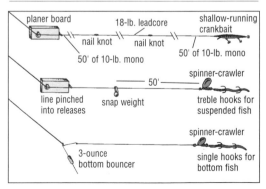

Trolling Riprap For Walleyes

A NGLERS SING THE PRAISES OF man-made rock structure in regions where soft-bottomed reservoirs offer little or no natural walleye spawning habitat. Rock riprap along the faces of dams and causeways creates what Mother Nature forgot to provide: suitable hard-bottomed spawning habitat washed by current, perfect for the deposition and oxygenation of walleye eggs, safe from predators until the fry hatch and scatter into the open-water surface layers of the main lake. This is the ideal spring fish attractor once water temperatures approach the walleye's spawning range of around 45°F.

Trolling Riprap

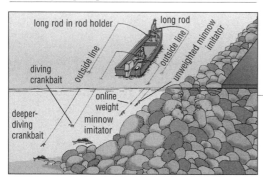

When— Water temperatures between 42°F and 55°F.

Tackle— *Rods:* 7- to 9-foot spinning or casting rods on outside lines and 5½- to 6-foot rods for inside lines. *Reels:* medium-capacity spinning or baitcasting reels. *Line:* 10-pound-test abrasion-resistant monofilament.

Rigging— The key to effective trolling is to stagger lines and lures at different depths to cover the sloping face of the dam or causeway. To best accomplish this, select lures that run at

Stagger lures to cover all depths while trolling. Select shallow runners for the inside shallower edge of the dam, diving crankbaits for the deeper outside edge. Pumping hand held rods usually triggers more fish than trolling with rods in holders.

a range of diving depths. Troll the shallowest versions closest to the dam, switching to deeper-running baits farther out. Use different rod lengths to spread lines on the same side of the boat. For example, on the line closest to the dam, long-line troll a shallow-running minnow imitator on a 7- to 9-foot rod. Then use a slightly deeper-running lure on the same side of the boat on a 5½- to 6-foot rod. Do the same on the opposite side of the boat, but consider the slope of the rock face and the lure's running depth to reach near or occasionally bounce bottom.

Presentation— When darkness falls, fish move shallow. Use an electric or small outboard motor to move just fast enough to wobble your crankbaits. Proceed parallel along the dam face in a straight path; weaving is unnecessary and usually counterproductive, since it takes baits over open water instead of skimming the face of the rocks. Occasional lure contact with the rocks is fine, but avoid pounding lures—sooner or later you'll snag. Pump handheld rods occasionally to add a stop-and-go action to lures, making them appear vulnerable or wounded to further enhance their attractiveness to walleyes. □

Top Spots On Riprap

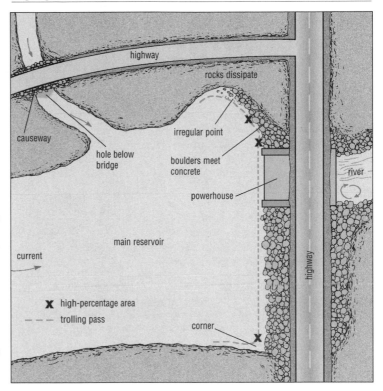

highway

rocks dissipate

irregular point

causeway

hole below bridge

boulders meet concrete

powerhouse

river

main reservoir

highway

current

X high-percentage area

- - - trolling pass

corner

Vertical Jigging For River Walleyes

3/8-ounce vertical jig

1-ounce thumper jig

1/16-ounce weedless pitchin' jig

THE WALLEYE RIVER MIGRATION begins in fall. Cooling water temperatures urge fish toward spring spawning sites. On large to medium-sized rivers, walleyes moving upstream encounter impassible barriers like dams. Their progress blocked, they fall back into the river section a mile or so downstream and assume feeding positions.

Boat Control

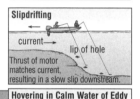

Slipdrifting

current →

lip of hole

Thrust of motor matches current, resulting in a slow slip downstream.

Hovering in Calm Water of Eddy

jigs

Anchoring

jigs

Cast downstream to fish and wait.

If the river is large enough and deep enough to permit passage beneath the ice, day after day, month after month, more fish arrive. Catching these fish requires vertical presentations along edges where current and slack water meet, or across areas of reduced current flow. The trick is to present slow-moving baits on or just off bottom and through prime feeding and holding areas. Tactics don't need to be fancy, but they must be on target. Missing by a few feet is as bad as missing by a mile.

When—

Tackle— *Rod:* 6-foot medium-light to medium-power fast-action spinning rod. *Reel:* medium-capacity spinning reel. *Line:* 6- to 8-pound-test mono.

Rigging—Jigs with round or oblong heads and weighing between 1/8 and 1/2 ounce cover most conditions. Fluorescent orange and chartreuse are more visible in dingy water, while whites and blacks trigger more strikes in clear water. Bladebaits and jigging spoons weighing 1/2 to 1 ounce also work.

bladebait

Presentation—

Boat control is critical. Most conditions call for a slow "slip" downstream, using motor thrusts against current to nearly neutralize drift speed. This tactic presents jigs, spoons, or bladebaits naturally, drifting downcurrent. Use a lift-drop-pause movement of your rod tip to give a 3- to 6-inch rise-fall action to the jig.

Around spawning time, high murky water begins to flood shoreline cover and pushes walleyes shallower. Maneuver into shoreline eddies and use your outboard or electric motor to neutralize river current and to hover in place. Consider anchoring on prime spots like eddies,

jigging
spoon

wing dams, or the lips of holes. Cast a jig out and let the current sweep it downstream. □

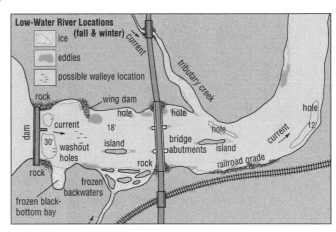

Low-Water River Locations (fall & winter)

ice

eddies

possible walleye location

tributary creek

rock

wing dam

hole

hole

hole

dam

current

18'

30'

washout holes

island

bridge abutments

hole

island

current

12'

railroad grade

rock

rock

frozen backwaters

frozen black-bottom bay

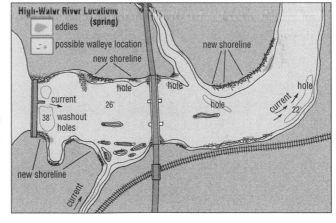

High-Water River Locations (spring)

eddies

possible walleye location

new shoreline

new shoreline

new shoreline

hole

hole

current

26'

38'

washout holes

hole

current

22'

new shoreline

current

Icing Yellow Perch

I N THE WATER, YELLOW PERCH ARE A challenge, especially jumbos weighing a pound or more. On the table, they're perfection. And they're fun to catch, too. The problem is finding them. Yellow perch are opportunists—some may hold near rock and gravel, while others are on sand or muck; some may be deep, while others are shallow. Perch usually relate to the bottom, but they also suspend. Perch also love to hold near weed-growth. With so many options available to the fish, focus on high-percentage spots and keep moving until you contact concentrations of fish.

When—

Tackle— *Rod:* 2- to 3-foot ultralight fast-action ice rod. *Reel:* small-capacity spinning reel. *Line:* 4-pound-test mono.

Rigging— Bigger and bolder is better to attract and then trigger perch in

Lures For Aggressive Perch In Deep Water

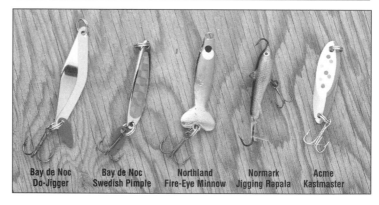

| Bay de Noc Do-Jigger | Bay de Noc Swedish Pimple | Northland Fire-Eye Minnow | Normark Jigging Rapala | Acme Kastmaster |

deep water. The depths are darker, so fish can't discriminate detail so well, and they aren't so harassed as fish in shallow water. These deep fish often are difficult to find, but relatively easy to catch with a handful of proven lures. Flash lures like 1/8- to 1/4-ounce jigging spoons, or swimming lures like a #3 or #5 Jigging Rapala, are the best choice when perch are aggressive. Tip the treble hook with maggots or a minnow head. When perch are picky, switch to a search lure like Custom Jigs and Spins' Slip Dropper rig tipped with 3 or 4 maggots. Make your own search lure by replacing the treble hook on a jigging spoon with 2½ inches of 4-pound-test line and a tiny jig.

***Location*—** Perch prefer ranging on flats and tend not to hold on drop-offs. Once perch slide off shallow flats, they usually drop all the way to the base of the drop-off, and range in the area of the drop-off—particularly in the section where the transition from harder to softer bottom begins. This transition usually occurs within 50 yards of the base of the drop-off. Target the 100-yard zone beginning at the base of the drop-off and running into the basin.

Perch often roam in groups that may cover several hundred yards and include hundreds or even thousands of fish. It's not difficult to find them, however, if you search systematically. A group of three anglers, for example, can quickly search a large area by drilling holes perpendicular to the basin edge.

Drop a bait down to the bottom, do some aggressive jigging, and watch your electronics for signs of fish. Give a hole three minutes, then move further down the edge.

***Presentation*—** Aggressive jigging, that is, quick lift-falls of a foot or more, attract fish— bring them in for a closer look at the bait. Watch for fish on sonar. When a fish moves in, jiggle the rod tip so the jig quivers in place, then stop. When the fish moves in closer, give another little jiggle and stop again. Often fish in deep water will immediately move in and inhale the bait. If there's any hesitation, slowly jiggle the bait as you raise it a couple inches. If the fish still refuses to take, resume aggressive jigging to call in another fish. □

Beginning Of The Basin

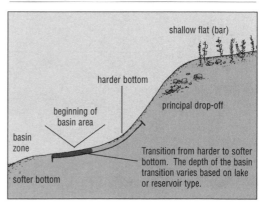

shallow flat (bar)

harder bottom

principal drop-off

beginning of basin area

basin zone

Transition from harder to softer bottom. The depth of the basin transition varies based on lake or reservoir type.

softer bottom

Probing Weedlines For Yellow Perch

THE WEEDLINE IS AN INTERFACE between two worlds. Blue expanses, deep structure, and basin flats are present on one side of this green dimension, while shallow, fertile flats extend to shore on the other. In most lakes, most perch will opt for deep water. But some use weed flats and weededges all summer, then move deep as winter approaches, following the warmest water, which is present in basins after turnover. Even though shallow fish tend to scatter along weededges, this pattern remains one of the easiest ways to locate catchable numbers. In many places, a daily limit of perch is 25, and that many can easily be caught on weededges in an afternoon.

When— 🌷 ☀ 🍂

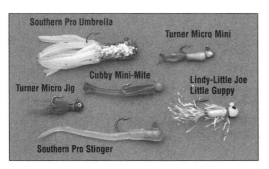

Southern Pro Umbrella

Turner Micro Mini

Cubby Mini-Mite

Turner Micro Jig

Lindy-Little Joe Little Guppy

Southern Pro Stinger

Tackle— *Rod:* 6- to 7-foot light-power spinning rod. *Reel:* medium-capacity spinning reel. *Line:* 2- or 4-pound-test mono.

Rigging— Keep your lure options simple. Casting a 1/32-ounce jig tipped with a crayfish tail or piece of crawler, or a small spinner rig baited with a small leech or red worm will catch most of the perch you encounter.

Location—Throughout the day, perch often maintain positions just inside the weededge or right at the base of the weeds. They may also bunch up in specific spots on the adjacent flat, but these fish are harder to locate and keep up with. Look for irregularities in the weedline. A gravel or rock finger extending from an open pocket in the weeds, an inside turn at the base of a point in the weedline, or a change in density or type of weedgrowth attracts more perch and holds them longer.

Presentation—First casts determine the layout of the weededge. Next, cast over the weeds. Swim the jig over the weed tops and drop it down the edge. Crappies might hold on top of the weeds, but perch usually strike as the jig drops to the base of the weeds. Then cast parallel to the edge and let the jig fall all the way to the bottom before lift-dropping it back along the edge. Move the boat to the edge of your previous casting range and repeat the presentation sequence. □

Working A Weedline

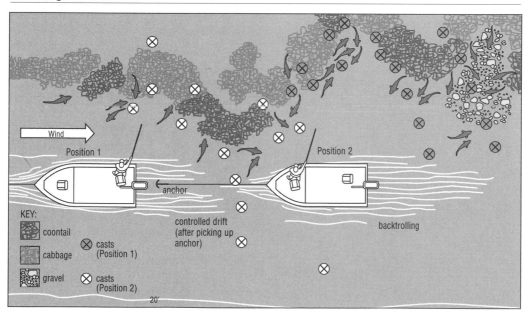

KEY:
coontail
cabbage
gravel
⊗ casts (Position 1)
⊗ casts (Position 2)

Wind
Position 1
Position 2
anchor
controlled drift (after picking up anchor)
backtrolling
20'

Where And How To Catch Saugeye

W HAT DO YOU GET WHEN YOU MIX a walleye's penchant for growing big with a sauger's fondness for dirty water? The saugeye—a hybrid created by crossing a female walleye with a male sauger. Often confused with their parental species, saugeyes typically have dark brown backs with darker saddle-shaped markings like a sauger, and a white tip on the lower tip of the tail like a walleye. Saugeyes also have a continuous black blotch at the base of the dorsal fin, while sauger have rows of distinct black spots. These mud-loving fish are gaining popularity with fishery managers looking for stocking options and anglers seeking fast action and big fish.

Saugeye Distribution

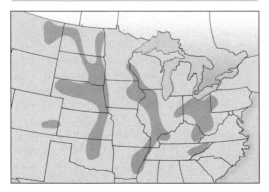

When—

Tackle— *Rod:* 6- to 7½-foot fast-action spinning rod. *Reel:* medium-capacity spinning reel with a long-casting spool. *Line:* 8- to 12-pound-test mono.

Location— Saugeye are more tolerant of warm water than walleyes, and are particularly suited to life in turbid reservoirs. While they usually don't reproduce with another saugeye, they are not a sterile hybrid and are capable of reproducing with either parent stock. Saugeyes often run upriver in winter and spring, stacking in tailwaters below dams. As the water warms in late spring, many disperse back downstream into shallow, turbid reservoirs. In muddy reservoirs without much current, riprap areas along the face of the lower dam may attract and concentrate spawning saugeyes when the water temperature reaches the mid-40°F to mid-50°F range. Later in the season, prominent structures meeting the old river channel are key spots. Focus on the drop-off edge, but don't be afraid to fish shallow flats, particularly if the water's muddy.

Typical Saugeye Reservoir

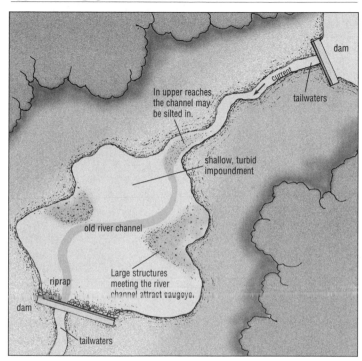

In upper reaches, the channel may be silted in.

shallow, turbid impoundment

old river channel

Large structures meeting the river channel attract saugeye.

riprap

dam

tailwaters

dam

current

tailwaters

Presentation—Most classic walleye rigs and presentations work for saugeyes, but jigs tipped with livebait are particularly effective. Starting at ice-out, drift minnow-tipped jigs close to the bottom. Like saugers, saugeyes often ignore a bait presented more than a few inches off the bottom, so use enough weight to maintain bottom contact. As fish move into their summer locations, drift jigs tipped with a piece of night crawler across rocky points and reefs. Numbers of fish have been caught by trolling crankbaits around points above the thermocline. In other regions, shorecasting weighted minnowbaits just before dark has produced enough state-record-class fish to quickly become the favorite big-fish technique. □

Finding Sauger

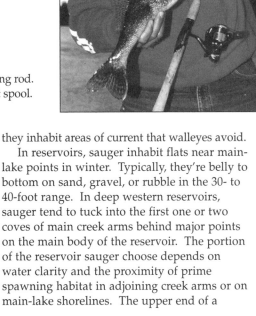

SAUGER ARE COMMON IN MANY RIVERINE environments throughout the natural and extended range of their larger cousin, the walleye. Unlike walleye, however, sauger often are ignored. Worse, they're sometimes considered a nuisance. If you've never given sauger a fair chance, here are a couple of reasons to reconsider. They bite well when walleyes won't. And they bite aggressively. Before you can catch them, though, you have to find them.

When—

Tackle— *Rod:* 6- to 6½-foot medium-power spinning rod. *Reel:* medium-capacity spinning reel with a long-cast spool. *Line:* 6- to 10-pound-test abrasion-resistant mono.

Location— Big sauger in rivers don't hold with the small boys. Smaller sauger generally inhabit the deepest available pools, holes, or main-river basin areas. Bigger sauger (over 3 pounds) cruise the same haunts walleyes frequent, but arrive and feed on these spots early or late in the day, or for more extended periods on nasty, windy, precipitous days. Look for the biggest sauger at the head of structural elements like gravel bars, sand bars, points, holes, and humps. They also hold to the current side of structural elements more than walleyes do, and

they inhabit areas of current that walleyes avoid.

In reservoirs, sauger inhabit flats near main-lake points in winter. Typically, they're belly to bottom on sand, gravel, or rubble in the 30- to 40-foot range. In deep western reservoirs, sauger tend to tuck into the first one or two coves of main creek arms behind major points on the main body of the reservoir. The portion of the reservoir sauger choose depends on water clarity and the proximity of prime spawning habitat in adjoining creek arms or on main-lake shorelines. The upper end of a reservoir tends to be the most turbid, but the best spawning habitat may be nearer the dam.

***Presentation*—** The biggest sauger in any given area tend to position in or near slight to moderate current at the head of structures. If possible, position the boat by anchoring abreast of these key locations. Cast above and beyond them, dragging or popping the jig downstream and across the element, which keeps the jig in the sauger's line of vision for the longest possible time. Where current allows, positioning with a trolling motor while casting works as well or better. In reservoirs, dragging a jig across the flats usually triggers more fish. Experiment with erratic retrieves, but keep your jig moving slowly on or just above the bottom where sauger feed. ☐

Location In Rivers

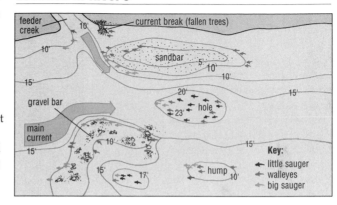

Location In Reservoirs

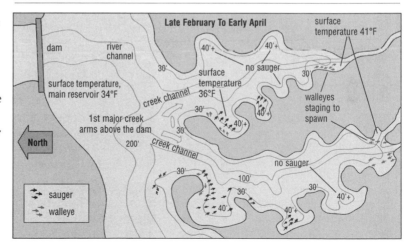

Icing Big Bluegills

BLUEGILLS ARE SO WIDELY DISTRIBUTED and bite so consistently that most anglers have good bluegill fishing available all year. Sure, there are difficult days, and fishing for trophy bluegills is often as tough as trying to tag a 30-pound muskie. But bluegills of one size or another usually cooperate if you work at it. This is especially true during the winter, when bluegills feed heavily on zooplankton. They must feed often to sustain themselves on tiny bits of protein, making them catchable for extended periods.

When—

Tackle— *Rod:* 2- to 3-foot ultralight-power ice rod. *Reel:* ultralight spinning reel or plastic ice-fishing reel. *Line:* 1- to 4-pound-test limp mono.

Basic Jigging

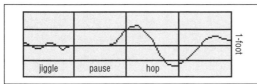

A good Daphnia jigging imitation is a subtle 1/8-inch fluttering movement. Inject larger hops into the jigging sequence to attract bluegills from a distance, then pause to trigger interested fish.

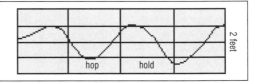

Copepods are more difficult for bluegills to catch, but are more available at midday when other zooplankton move deep. The basic darter-imitating jigging movement is a hop, hold, hop, hold.

Location— Shallow weedgrowth is the most consistent, basic bluegill pattern. But for consistent fishing, it's important to find weeds on a large bar, or in a large bay with extensive summer weedgrowth. The remaining healthy weeds usually attract and hold bluegills all winter. While the largest members of the bluegill population also are attracted to weeds, they're as likely to be rock-oriented. Larger fish also tend to hold in deeper water, at times as deep as 30 feet.

Presentation— Tear drops and leadhead jigs imitate microscopic animals that bluegills feed on. The many types of plankton can be classified into two categories: darters like copepods, and bobbers and flutterers like Daphnia. Besides their different appearance, each animal has characteristic movements and environmental requirements. Daphnia swim slowly in a bobbing fashion and tend to slowly migrate upward in the water column at dark, downward in daylight. Copepods are built for bursts of speed and also can swim erratically. They often hold an established position regardless of light conditions, although general movements up or down or left or right may take place on a daily or weekly basis. Let the fish determine which presentation you use by seeing how they respond to variations of each approach. ☐

Tipping Tips

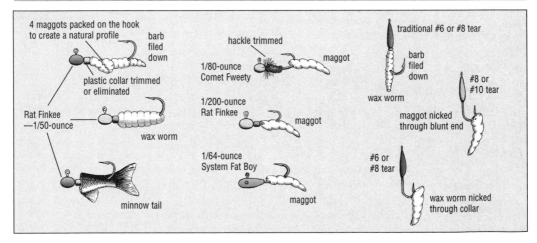

4 maggots packed on the hook to create a natural profile

barb filed down

plastic collar trimmed or eliminated

Rat Finkee —1/50-ounce

wax worm

minnow tail

hackle trimmed

maggot

1/80-ounce Comet Fweety

1/200-ounce Rat Finkee

maggot

1/64-ounce System Fat Boy

maggot

traditional #6 or #8 tear

barb filed down

wax worm

#8 or #10 tear

maggot nicked through blunt end

#6 or #8 tear

wax worm nicked through collar

Evaluating Bluegills In Ponds

PONDS ARE THE MOST NUMEROUS fishing waters in the U.S., with about 1,000 new ones built each year in states within the "pond belt," roughly extending from northern Virginia west to southern Montana and including regions south of that line. But even outside this zone, some states contain tens of thousands of ponds. In fact, statistics suggest that dozens of ponds lie within a 10-mile radius of most anglers, except where large lakes dominate the landscape. Your best chance to catch a 1-pound bluegill may be to find the most productive ponds in your neighborhood and gain access to them.

When—

Tackle— *Rod:* 5- to 7-foot light-power spinning rod. *Reel:* small spinning reel with a long-cast spool. *Line:* 2- to 6-pound-test mono.

Pond Potential—The key to picking a productive pond is to find out how the pond is managed. While bluegills are one of the most popular pond species, finding ponds that contain many fish over half a pound can be challenging. When bluegill numbers rise, their growth rates fall as they compete for food. Stunting can occur if bass or other predators aren't abundant.

If you fish an unmanaged pond, look for clues to its condition. Abundant small bass suggest that bluegills will be large, unless they've been harvested heavily. Bass fishing for larger fish will be poor, although a couple giants may reside there, if it's a mature pond. Many small bait-stealing bluegills indicate their overabundance, probably due to overharvest of bass. Forget this pond.

Location— Farm ponds with shallow, featureless basins are dug with earth-moving equipment and filled from runoff of the adjacent watershed. Although most dug ponds are less than 5 acres, fertilization can greatly improve their productivity. Bluegills often gather under overhanging trees to eat insects, or in shade from shoreline trees and bushes. During summer, deep areas may lack oxygen and fish avoid them.

Building a dam across a low area backs up runoff, forming a built pond

Dug Pond

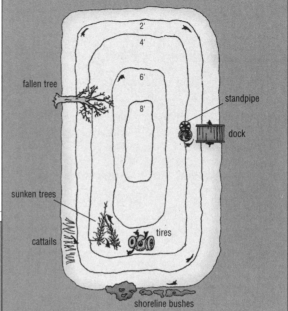

fallen tree

standpipe

dock

sunken trees

cattails

tires

shoreline bushes

Built Pond

Funnels are high-percentage spots.

cut

4'

6'

weedbed

10'

8'

wintering area

cut

lying logs

stumps

tires

emergency spillway

point

fallen tree

from 2 to 50 acres. The area near the dam is deepest, with gradually shallower water toward the opposite end. Cuts, points, humps, and flats with weeds or timber attract bluegills. During summer, gills may cruise open water to feed on zooplankton or hold near emergent vegetation and submerged weedlines. □

Spawn-Time Bluegills

A S WATER TEMPERATURES PUSH
toward 65 °F, bluegills move toward potential spawning areas. Groups of bluegills scatter
across flats, usually holding near weed cover.
Under stable weather and rising water temperature, they may also roam shallow, searching for
areas of favored bottom type ranging from fine
sand mixed with silt to coarse gravel. These bedding colonies provide easy fishing. And because
it's adults-only, large fish are more concentrated
than at any other time of year.

When—

*Livebait and flies are fine options for bedding
bluegills. But when fish are aggressive, nothing
beats small leadhead jigs with tube or twistertail
bodies. A drop of glue keeps plastic bodies from
sliding off the jig, while floats and casting bubbles
increase casting distance and bite detection.*

Tackle—*Rod:* 6- to 12-foot light-power spinning rod or 10- to 20-foot pole. *Reel:* lightweight spinning reel. *Line:* 4- or 6-pound-test limp mono.

Rigging—Bait choice isn't critical. Crickets and red worms are popular throughout the South, while maggots and leeches are often used in the North. Big bluegills also like tiny jigs, plain or tipped with a maggot or piece of night crawler. Suspend baits beneath a sensitive float to detect subtle strikes.

Location—Monitor water temperature to determine when to begin searching for spawning fish. Search sheltered coves, creek arms, or channels where temperatures are higher than in the main body of water. In rivers, look for sloughs or oxbows with slack current—current on the nest can smother the eggs with silt, so bluegills avoid it.

Bluegills generally nest close to shore, in depths that allow nests to be seen from a boat or shore. In areas that appear to offer appropriate water temperature, shelter, and bottom type, look for pale

circles 8 to 12 inches in diameter. Anchoring allows the quickest and most efficient fishing from a boat. Wading is also productive.

Presentation—Male bluegills rarely feed during the spawn, but instinctively strike livebaits and small jigs presented near nests. Fish slightly deeper near bedding colonies for prespawn females and males between nesting efforts. If you spook fish from a spawning area, back off and they'll return. If you're one of the first anglers to fish a spawning colony, it's often easy to catch 5 or 10 fish before they become wary. ☐

Bluegill Spawning Locations

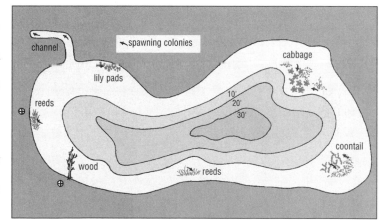

The population of spawning bluegills in ponds, lakes, and reservoirs is often so large that the fish don't all fit into one or two spots. Look for shallow areas that provide a suitable bottom and protective cover.

Finding Postspawn Bluegills

BLUEGILLS SPAWN WHEN WATER temperature ranges from about 67°F to 74°F, then they scatter. Males may linger near spawning habitat for a few days, but females move quickly into postspawn patterns. They may suspend over deep water, following wind-driven plankton. Or, more often, they inhabit both shallow and deep weedlines, rock piles, or humps. Finding a few bluegills is seldom a problem, but finding concentrations—especially big fish—is a matter of keying on prime postspawn patterns.

When—

Tackle— *Rod:* 5- to 7-foot light-power spinning rod. *Reel:* lightweight spinning reel with long-cast spool. *Line:* 2- to 6-pound-test limp mono. □

Summary Bluegill Patterns

Legend:
- bluegills
- pads
- cabbage-coontail beds
- sparse cabbage on hard bottom
- rock
- junk weed

Spawning (67°F to 74°F) often takes place in areas of slightly harder bottom. Larger 'gills may spawn in deeper water. In clear water, 'gills may spawn 8 to 12 feet down.

Deep pads attract some fish.

37'

After spawning (+74°F) big bluegills migrate to deep weedlines and offshore humps.

hard-bottom hump

When forage thins along deep weed-lines, some bluegills suspend, following wind-blown clouds of plankton (midsummer, usually over 72°F)

27'

15'

By midsummer to late summer, some of the biggest bluegills migrate to main-lake weedlines, points, and humps. The best main-lake locations generally are near fertile bays or part of the most fertile segment of the lake—fertile meaning they offer soft bottom and weedgrowth.

wind

Summer Period (70°F to 82°F)

plankton

suspended fish

Three major patterns:
- deep weedlines
- rocky humps (or weed humps in deep water)
- suspended fish following wind-blown plankton

lowlight periods

12'

daytime

deep rockpile

25'

Summer Patterns For Big Bluegills

THE HUNT FOR TROPHY PREDATORY fish like bass, walleye, and pike is a process. Good fishermen start with the most likely pattern, given the time of year, then move on to the next, systematically eliminating unproductive water and techniques. Many bluegill fishermen, on the other hand, are stuck in a rut. They anchor on the same weedbed they've been fishing for years and haul out the worms and bobbers. But big bluegills are more likely roaming open water than mingling with peanut panfish in the weeds. And catching them requires a different approach.

When—

Tackle— *Rod:* 5- to 7-foot light-power spinning rod. *Reel:* lightweight spinning reel with long-cast spool. *Line:* 2- to 6-pound-test limp mono.

Presentation— Large lakes with lots of deep open water areas often grow the biggest bluegills. On a typical summer day, consider 6 basic patterns.

Pockets on Flats—Look for weed flats with gravel or rocky areas forming pockets with multiple edges. Pockets also form where low weeds meet high weeds, where pads meet reeds or coontail, and around weed clumps. These areas suggest variations in bottom content and multiple food sources like nymphs, snails, and leeches.

Deep Weededges—Look for the outside or deep edge of the weedline. Predators prowl here, so only the biggest bluegills stay. Wind-driven plankton is corralled by the weed wall. Multiple forage types make these edges good all year.

Deep-Lying Rocks—Look for rocky drop-offs. Check shallow on rock slides as well as the deep-lying base of a slide. Or look for rock piles on flats 15 to 40 feet deep. These bulls feed on small crustaceans, nematodes, nymphs, and other organisms.

Hard-Bottom Humps—Look for submerged islands and humps with gravel or marl. Big bluegills find crawling and burrowing nymphs or aquatic worms in mud, sand, or marl on top of those elements.

Open Water—A wind shift away from a weedline moves plankton over open water. Big gills follow if plankton are plentiful. Bluegills stay above the thermocline, typically concentrating 10 to 18 feet down.

Terrestrials—Look for insects like grass-hoppers blown onto the lake. Bulls from the flats and weedline move shallow in the evening or during the day when offshore winds are strongest. Bluegills feeding on plankton may switch to this pattern if zooplankton decline in late summer. □

Common Summer Bluegill Patterns

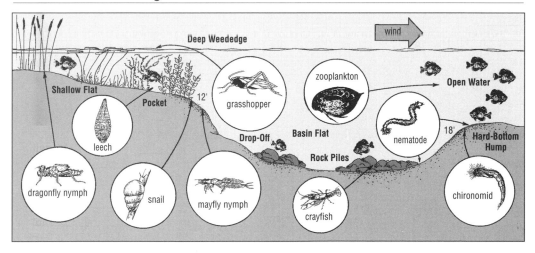

Crappies During The Fall Transition

I N THE NORTH COUNTRY, CRAPPIES begin their great locational shift in September, as water temperature drops into the mid-60°F range. This shift may not be completed until late November in the deep South. While the motivation for the shift isn't fully understood, it is recognized by crappie experts throughout the country. During summer, the thermocline marks the lower boundary of crappie domain. Cool water below the thermocline may be attractive to crappies, but the level of dissolved oxygen can't support them. As fall progresses, the thermocline disintegrates, the lower water level is reoxygenated, and crappies are free to use deeper water.

When—

Tackle— *Rod:* 6- to 8-foot light-power spinning rod. *Reel:* small-capacity spinning reel. *Line:* 6- to 10-pound-test mono, depending on cover.

Rigging— For vertical jigging, especially in or along the edges of standing timber, use 1/16-, 1/8-, or 1/4-ounce jigs with compact heads and small grub bodies. The weight of these lures is sufficient to maintain contact at depths down to 50 feet. They allow precise vertical presentation and won't swim so erratically as a light tube jig.

Double Jig Rig

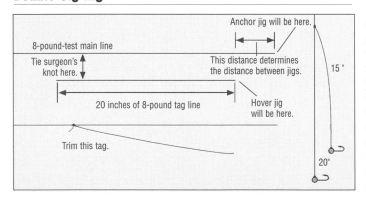

8-pound-test main line

Tie surgeon's knot here.

20 inches of 8-pound tag line

Trim this tag.

Anchor jig will be here.

This distance determines the distance between jigs.

Hover jig will be here.

15"

20"

Location—In early fall in reservoirs, many crappies are in the upper ends of major creek arms and feeder creeks, where mid-depth cover ranges 8 to 20 feet deep, and shad or other baitfish are abundant. Look for brushy channel edges or timbered points that slope toward the creek channel. As water temperature falls into the upper 50°F range, crappies gradually shift downstream to deeper points along channels.

As water cools in natural lakes, much of the weedgrowth on flats dies, although some deep-lying weeds usually remain along drop-offs. Crappies holding on shallow flats shift to join crappies already holding along drop-off edges. Crappies holding in open water do the same. Once crappies are along edges, they may continue to hold along the deep edge of remaining weedgrowth or drop much deeper when rock cover lies in deeper water.

Presentation—Find key areas by surveying with electronics. Often it's possible to see crappies holding relative to cover. A quick drop with a jig often confirms how active the fish are. Slowly troll along the edges of timber or slowly drift jigs along the edge of stump flats. When you catch fish you also see on sonar, stop and fish a double jig rig vertically. Use sonar to stay on top of the fish and to keep jigs at the proper depth. □

Typical Holding Patterns In Lakes

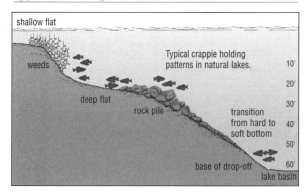

shallow flat

weeds

Typical crappie holding patterns in natural lakes.

deep flat

rock pile

transition from hard to soft bottom

base of drop-off

lake basin

10'
20'
30'
40'
50'
60'

Typical Holding Patterns In Reservoirs

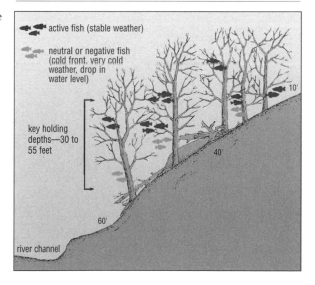

active fish (stable weather)

neutral or negative fish (cold front, very cold weather, drop in water level)

key holding depths—30 to 55 feet

10'
40'
60'

river channel

CRAPPIE

Night Bite Crappies

M ANY CRAPPIE ANGLERS concentrate on spring prespawn and spawning fish in shallow coves and creek arms. As male crappies guard hatching fry, females disperse toward open water. Males follow as soon as their parental duties are complete. But as fishing pressure on crappies increases, most anglers continue to ignore an important fact—throughout most of the season, night is the best time to catch crappies. These bug-eyed predators see well after dark and take advantage of nocturnal prey movements to feed efficiently.

When—

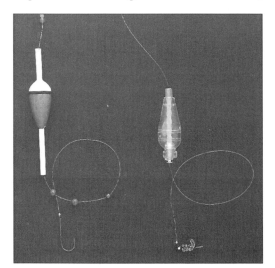

Tackle— *Rod:* 6- to 7-foot light-power spinning rod. *Reel:* small-capacity spinning reel. *Line:* 4- to 8-pound-test mono.

Rigging— Livebait or jigs suspended below slip floats are effective night rigs. Tie a stop knot on your main line, followed by a bead and a small, narrow slipfloat. The float should be sensitive enough to balance with a few small shot so it can easily be pulled under by a light-biting crappie. Light-wire #6 to #1 hooks keep small minnows alive and active, and they hook crappies firmly. Popular baits vary by region, but fathead minnows are tough to beat for numbers of fish. Use medium-size shiners to attract large crappies.

Location—At night, crappies move toward the surface and gather to feed below schools of baitfish. Find a concentration of active crappies at night, and you'll experience some of the finest fishing in freshwater. Large main-lake points and the mouths of large creeks often attract large schools of shad and crappies. Bridges are another good area to intercept nocturnal crappies. The riprapped banks, old abutments, and lights associated with bridges attract plankton and baitfish, and in turn, crappies. On populated lakes, lighted docks also attract crappie and their prey. In clear water, docks standing in at least five feet of water produce best, while crappies in murky water often move much shallower.

Presentation—Once you locate crappies, catching them isn't difficult. Slowly cruising around an area while watching your electronics often reveals the presence of crappies and their forage. Set your float stop to suspend your bait slightly above the fish and cast into the fray. If the action stops during the night, check the area with sonar or adjust your stop knot before moving to another spot. Shad and other baitfish often follow clouds of plankton by making vertical movements throughout the night, and crappies likely follow. □

Boat Docks

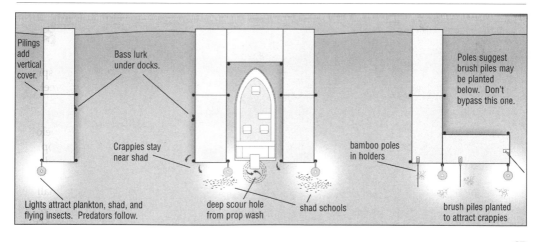

Pilings add vertical cover.

Bass lurk under docks.

Poles suggest brush piles may be planted below. Don't bypass this one.

Crappies stay near shad

bamboo poles in holders

Lights attract plankton, shad, and flying insects. Predators follow.

deep scour hole from prop wash

shad schools

brush piles planted to attract crappies

Pole Tactics For Crappies

TAKE-A-PART GRAPHITE

N
ORTH AMERICAN ANGLERS ARE
blessed with almost unlimited mobility.
Widespread public access and the availability of
boats and sophisticated electronics have resulted in
fishing systems that quickly eliminate unproductive water. Most presentations are geared toward
fish in aggressive or neutral feeding moods. In
contrast, European anglers have little access or
mobility and have developed refined light-tackle
systems to trigger spooky fish. You don't need 33-
foot poles, 1-pound-test line, and #24 hooks to
catch crappies, but modified approaches—hybrids
of American and European tactics—often produce
lots of fish in hard-to-reach areas.

When—

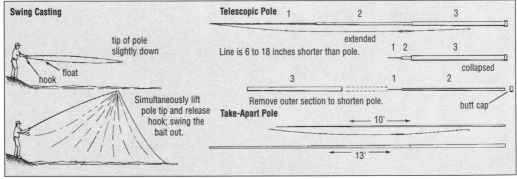

Swing Casting

tip of pole
slightly down

float

hook

Simultaneously lift
pole tip and release
hook; swing the
bait out.

Telescopic Pole 1 2 3

extended
Line is 6 to 18 inches shorter than pole.

1 2 3

collapsed

3 1 2

Remove outer section to shorten pole. **Take-Apart Pole**

butt cap

← 10' →

← 13' →

Tackle—*Pole:* 15- to 30-foot telescopic or take-apart pole. *Line:* 2- to 6-pound-test mono.

Rigging—Both telescopic and take-apart poles are simple and fun to use, particularly when they're constructed from strong, lightweight graphite or graphite-composite materials. Telescopic poles usually are more flexible than take-apart poles and are easier to use. Rig your line so the hook rides 6 to 18 inches shorter than the length of the pole. Rig long take-apart poles the same as telescopic poles, or use a short 4- to 6-foot line for better control in wind and waves.

Use a plummet or ice-fishing depthfinder to determine the depth of the water and layout of the cover. Next, rig a small fixed float on the line and add enough lead shot to balance the float so only a small portion of the tip extends above the surface of the water. Hook small minnows parallel to the dorsal fin with a #6 to #12 light wire hook, or through the lips on a small jig. □

Pole Tactics

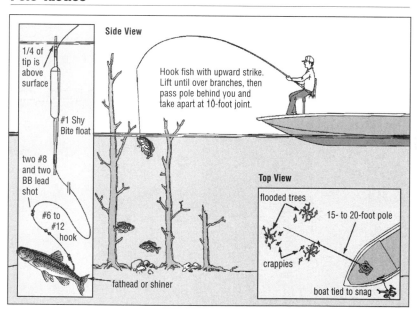

Side View

1/4 of tip is above surface

Hook fish with upward strike. Lift until over branches, then pass pole behind you and take apart at 10-foot joint.

#1 Shy Bite float

two #8 and two BB lead shot

#6 to #12 hook

fathead or shiner

Top View

flooded trees

15- to 20-foot pole

crappies

boat tied to snag

Suspender Floating For Ice Time Crappies

SUSPENDER FLOATING suits the middle of the ice-fishing season. First ice is long past and catching fish is more difficult. Better times are coming, but the last-ice binge is at least a month away. Suspender floating often turns a tough outing into a relative success; that is, a few crappies instead of none, and a few more fish when you would have caught some. All you need is a float rig weighted with enough lead shot to make the rig barely heavier than neutrally buoyant.

When—

Tackle— *Rod:* 2- to 3-foot ultralight ice rod. *Reel:* ultralight spinning reel or plastic ice reel.

Shot Setting

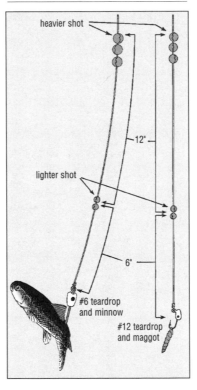

heavier shot

12"

lighter shot

6"

#6 teardrop and minnow

#12 teardrop and maggot

Line: 27-pound-test dacron main line and 4-pound-test mono leader.

Rigging—A dacron main line lets you hand-over-hand the rig to quickly land fish and get back down to the appropriate depth again. Tie a stop knot onto the dacron, and add a small bead and a slip float. Next, tie on a 3-foot section of 4-pound-test mono for your leader, and add enough lead shot to barely sink the float. Minnows can be fished on a plain hook, but a wide-gapped teardrop jig adds color and anchors the minnow, making it easier for crappie to catch. Barely nick the hook under the minnow's dorsal fin with the hook point pointing toward the minnow's head. Drop down to a #12 teardrop packed with maggots to trigger fish in a negative feeding mood.

Presentation—Drop the bait and shot down the hole. As it settles, set the float on the surface. Water tension on the surface of a properly balanced float will keep it from sinking. Move the float, however, and it will slowly begin to sink, along with the bait suspended below it. A slight jiggle of your rod tip adds an enticing movement to the bait that can't be duplicated with any other presentation.

If you see crappies on your sonar unit 5 to 10 feet off the bottom, set your float so the bait is suspended 8 feet above the bottom when the float is on the surface. This lets you fish the float from the surface down 3 feet—your bait 8 feet above bottom down to 5 feet above bottom. Cover more water by including a lift 3 feet above the water, then slowly dropping the float back down to the surface. □

Minnow Line Settings

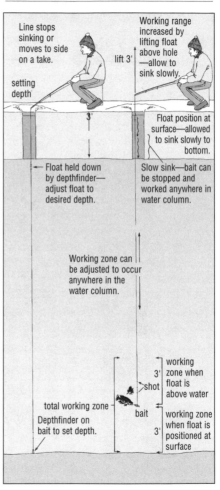

Trolling For Crappies

W HEN WARMING TRENDS HEAT THE back ends of shallow coves and creek arms in spring, crappies in lakes and reservoirs begin filtering into shallow cover to feed, then to spawn. For most crappie fishermen, the early season begins with that first startling visage of calico slabs hovering in the embrace of wood near shore. But some crappie fishermen have learned how to jump the gun on this traditional opener.

Discovering that crappies stage and suspend in open water adjacent to early spring feeding sites, these anglers troll a spread of diving minnow-baits on flatlines and planer boards.

Three-Way Trolling Rig

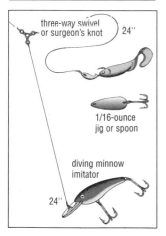

three-way swivel or surgeon's knot 24"

1/16-ounce jig or spoon

diving minnow imitator

24"

When—

Tackle— *Rod:* 6- to 7-foot medium-light-power spinning rod. *Reel:* small-capacity spinning reel. *Line:* 4- or 6-pound-test mono

Rigging— Running a spread of four lines— a planer board line on each side of the boat and

Small divers, minnowbaits, jigs, and spoons can easily be presented on 4-pound line with Big Jon's Mini Otter trolling boards.

two flatlines straight out the back—allows you to cover water quickly and efficiently as you search for active fish. Small crankbaits and minnowbaits are effective, but rigging these baits in tandem with jigs and spoons often triggers more fish. Tie a three-way swivel to your main line and attach two 24-inch leaders to the remaining swivel loops. To one leader attach a diving lure designed to reach a depth just above the level where fish are holding. Tie a 1/16-ounce jig or small spoon to the other leader.

Location— In hill-land reservoirs, crappies migrate up creek arms to suspend and stage. Classic location is in the back one-third of the arm. Specific areas are determined by a variety of comfort factors, including depth, forage, water clarity, and temperature. In lakes, crappies move into shallow bays, coves, and boat channels to feed in early spring. During warm, stable weather, they relate to shallow shoreline cover. Cold fronts move them back outside shallow bays or to the center of deeper

Suspension Zone In A Hill-Land Reservoir

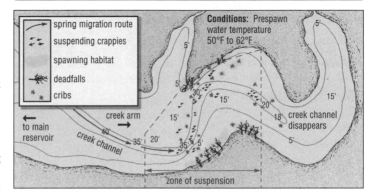

Suspension Zones In Lakes

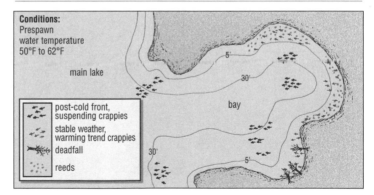

bays with at least a 25-foot maximum depth. Locating suspended crappies is the same in either environment—move slowly through bays or creek arms as you watch the depthfinder. ☐

All About Redear & Redbreast Sunfishes

Redear Sunfish—

The redear sunfish, widely known as "shellcracker" to anglers, is the largest member of the sunfish clan. They originally ranged from North Carolina and Florida west to Texas and southern Missouri. They're easy to identify with their bright yellow belly and sides, and bright red tab on the end on the gill flap. Introductions have expanded their range north and west. Shallow lakes, rivers, and reservoirs with abundant weeds are prime habitat.

Shellcrackers eat a variety of invertebrates, but get their name from their preference for snails, mussels, and clams, which they crunch with molarlike teeth located on their gill arches. They tend to feed on the bottom more than do other sunfish. They also are notoriously finicky

Joe Tomelleri

biters, often falling only for natural baits presented stealthily on light line with minimal terminal tackle. Some redear specialists troll unweighted gobs of red worms 100 to 150 feet behind a boat equipped with a quiet electric motor.

Spawning time, which usually coincides with the initial bluegill spawn, provides the fastest fishing. This occurs in late February in southern Florida and in June in southern Wisconsin and Pennsylvania. Big shellcrackers can, however, be taken throughout summer along weed stalks that hold small snails and over deeper edges of productive flats that offer hard-bottom areas attractive to mussels and clams.

Joe Tomelleri

Redbreast Sunfish— The redbreast sunfish is found in Atlantic Coast drainages from Maine to Florida and west along the Gulf Coast to Texas. They occupy diverse waters, from cold mountain streams to brackish coastal marshes, but reach a maximum size of about a pound in rivers. The redbreast is one of the most colorful North American freshwater fish, with fiery chest colors and variable blues, oranges, greens, and browns along the flanks. The color of the male redbreast intensifies during nest guarding.

Redbreasts have a large mouth and frequently snap jigs cast for smallmouths or minnowbaits twitched for large-mouths. But small spinners or jig-spinner combos like a 1/16-ounce Beetle Spin on ultralight tackle often work best. In rivers, look for redbreasts in slack water. Cypress trees, snags, and sandbars break current and provide shelter that redbreasts seek for feeding and spawning.

Redbreasts spawn later than most other sunfish—mid-April in Florida, June in the Mid-Atlantic states, and July in New England. They often build solitary nests close to shore and adjacent to logs, stumps, and snags, at depths from 1½ to 5 feet. Nests typically are large—about 3 feet in diameter and 6 to 8 inches deep. Their spawning also is less syn-chronized than other sunfish species, so while part of the population are on nests others will be preparing to spawn or moving into summer patterns. □

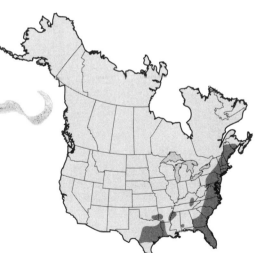

The Key To Pumpkinseed Sunfish

W HEREVER YOU LIVE, summertime is sunfish time. Time to relax and take the kids out for a fun time on the water. Whether it's a farm pond, small creek, reservoir, or lake, the members of the sunfish clan offer the fastest fishing of all. Much has been written about fishing techniques for bluegill, but other sunfish have been ignored. The aggressive nature, abundance, and large average size of the pumpkinseed, however, put them on par with any other panfish swimming.

When—

Tackle— *Rod:* 5½- to 7-foot light- or ultra-light-power spinning rod. *Reel:* small-capacity spinning reel. *Line:* 2- or 4-pound-test limp mono.

Rigging— Pumpkinseeds use flat teeth located in their throats to crush snails and other shelled invertebrates. Some biologists have even considered them a potential tool in the battle against invading zebra mussels. But they'll also take minnows and often bite large jigs and spinnerbaits targeting bass. The best baits for numbers of fish are natural baits like worms, grubs, and nymphs or small lures like spoons, spinners, and nymph-imitating flies fished near the bottom. A small clear casting bubble increases casting distance and allows weightless baits to drop slowly through the water column—a proven trigger of big pumpkinseeds.

Location— In northern waters from Maine and Nova Scotia to eastern North Dakota, and from Montana to Washington and British Columbia, pumpkinseeds cruise shallow flats, weedy bays, and slow rivers. Their native range also includes the Atlantic Coast states south to central Georgia, and midwestern states south to Illinois.

Distribution Of Pumpkinseed

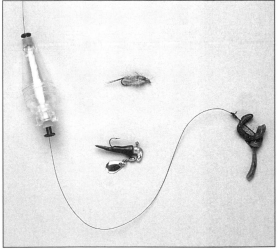

Presentation— Pumpkinseeds, especially larger ones, are most concentrated and accessible just before and during spawning. Like bluegills, pumpkinseeds move to spawning areas when water temperatures reach 68°F to 70°F. In the southern part of their range, this process may begin in late April or early May, and as late as mid- to late June in Canada. Pumpkinseed spawning colonies aren't so large as bluegill colonies, and solitary nests are common. Hybridization with bluegills sometimes occurs, producing an interestingly colored fertile hybrid possessing varying characteristics and the colors of either parent. □

Rock Bass Basics And Beyond

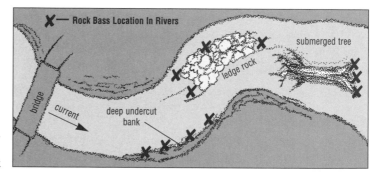

"RATS, IT'S ONLY A ROCKY!"
A familiar refrain across much of the rock bass range. They're not as tasty as yellow perch and they don't grow as large as walleyes, but they're one of the most aggressive fish in freshwater. They're plentiful, too, and they bite readily and put up a struggle on light tackle. In short, ol' goggle eyes is an untapped source of fishing fun for kids of all ages.

When—

a 1/2-ounce spinnerbait or an 8-inch plastic worm. Lures weighing 1/16 to 1/4 ounce, however, produce more fish. Top artificials include straight-shaft spinners, spinner and jig combos, and jigs. When the fishing's tough, try natural baits. Tie a #6 or #8 hook on your line and pinch on a shot or two 12 inches up. Bait with a hellgrammite, piece of night crawler, or crayfish tail.

Tackle— *Rod:* 6- to 7-foot light-power spinning rod. *Reel:* medium-capacity spinning reel. *Line:* 4- or 6-pound-test mono.

Rigging— Rock bass often are easy to catch because they're aggressive. It's not uncommon for a half-pound rockie to attack

✕— Rock Bass Location In Rivers

submerged tree

ledge rock

bridge

current

deep undercut bank

Location— Rock bass inhabit lakes, rivers, and reservoirs in the Midwest, East, and South-Central United States, and Southeast Canada. Fish for rockies in smallmouth-type habitat. In rivers, look for fish in deep pools, eddies, and current breaks formed by boulders and logs. In lakes, rock bass hold near rock and gravel areas. Rocky points, reefs, and sunken islands provide ideal habitat. Fish cribs and reed beds also attract rock bass. A few fish may be cruising deep weedlines with big sunfish.

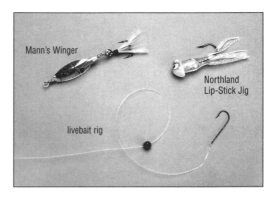

Mann's Winger

Northland Lip-Stick Jig

livebait rig

Presentation— In rivers, quarter casts upstream. Retrieve slowly, steering the lure around and through fish-holding cover. Active fish often are on the front edge of cover, ready to intercept food drifting in the current. Fish in a neutral mood may be positioned anywhere near cover in slack water. Catch these fish by probing cover with a lure tipped with bait. Lift the lure and let it fall into root tangles, under logs, and behind midstream boulders.

On lakes, a 1/8-ounce jig-worm combo fished on deep weededges is deadly for fish prowling the edge. Cast the jig into cuts and turns in the weed wall and let it sink to the bottom before beginning a slow retrieve. Or, cast small crankbaits parallel to the weeds. Work the bait erratically just above the bottom, moving along the edge until you contact fish. □

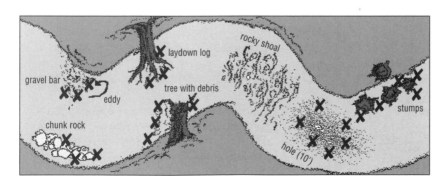

laydown log

rocky shoal

gravel bar

eddy

tree with debris

chunk rock

stumps

hole (10')

Ice-Fishing For Rainbow Trout

R AINBOW TROUT INHABIT THOUSANDS OF natural lakes from Maine to Washington, including the Great Lakes. They also thrive in many reservoirs, where ice-fishing often provides an overlooked opportunity. As cold-water fish, trout thrive under the ice and often prefer to feed in shallow water in winter—just the opposite of their summer preferences. The "reversal principle" allows various species to switch habitats throughout the year, preventing competition for the same forage at the same time. In winter, panfish often go deep while trout move shallow. In summer, they switch places. Successful ice-fishing depends on your ability to identify the areas active fish use during winter.

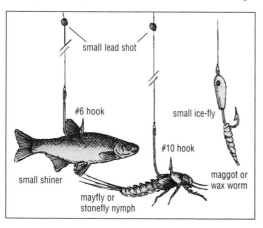

small lead shot

#6 hook

small ice-fly

#10 hook

small shiner

mayfly or stonefly nymph

maggot or wax worm

When—

Tackle— *Rod:* 2- to 3-foot medium-light-power ice rod. *Reel:* small-capacity spinning reel. *Line:* 4- or 6-pound-test mono.

Rigging—The best bait in natural lakes often is a live mayfly or stonefly nymph. Use light line, thin wire hooks or 1/125- to 1/80-ounce jigs, and a small lead shot 18 inches or so above the bait. Suspend the rig in the top half of the water column, since rainbows usually cruise above the bottom. In the Great Lakes and in larger reservoirs, minnows often are a top bait. Use a #6 Aberdeen hook and small lead shot or a jig in the 1/64- to 1/8-ounce range, depending on depth and size of the bait. Lip-hook or reverse-hook the minnow. Maggots and wax worms also work well on tiny jigs.

Location—One key to trout location in natural lakes is finding the largest shallow flats in the lake, since these areas tend to produce the most food. Bays and shoreline flats with a soft, sandy bottom or a variety of substrates are best for nymphs and larvae. Prime depths are 4 to 8 feet, unless no flats exist at those depths. Trout feed deeper, too, but when they do, it often occurs just past the lip of the first major drop leading to these shallow flats.

Presentation—Mobility often is a negative when fishing for rainbow trout in shallow water, since activity spooks them. Drill all your holes before sunrise. Scatter them over the flat and along the lip of the drop-off where the deepest water approaches closest to the flat. Trout rise from deeper adjacent flats at dawn, feed for several hours (well after noon on cloudy days), then drop back down. They return in the evening, and some continue feeding through the night. □

Winter Trout Location In Natural Lakes

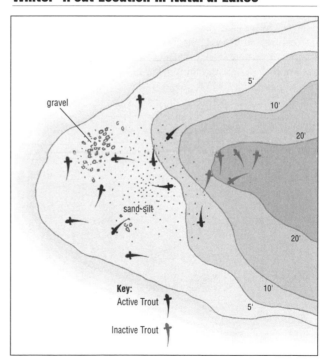

gravel

sand-silt

Key:
Active Trout

Inactive Trout

Trolling For Rainbow Trout In Still Waters

ACROSS THE UNITED STATES AND Canada, thousands of lakes and reservoirs have been stocked with rainbow trout. From small pits and ponds to massive reservoirs, these fisheries provide anglers with an opportunity for fast fishing. You need a basic understanding of rainbow trout location and a simple presentation system that puts your bait in front of as many fish as possible.

When—

Tackle— *Rod:* 6½- to 8-foot medium-power spinning or casting rod. *Reel:* medium-capacity spinning or baitcasting reel. *Line:* 8- to 12-pound-test mono.

Rigging— Keep your bait and presentation options for still-water rainbows as simple as possible. You'll catch trout by stillfishing or casting natural and artificial baits, but trolling often produces several more fish in the course of a day. Walleye-style livebait rigs can be used to present night crawlers, small minnows, and other natural baits, but the versatile three-way rig is a better option when fish are holding off the bottom. Livebait triggers neutral trout, but flatline trolling with spinners, spoons, minnowbaits, and flies attracts more strikes when fish are active.

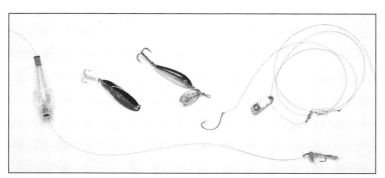

Location— Rainbows in lakes and reservoirs often elude anglers because they relate more to temperature bands than obvious structural elements. During spring and fall, they often hold just below the surface over deep water, but even during summer they're likely in the top 20 feet of the water column if a comfortable temperature range is available. Points, humps, and other structural elements that extend into water ranging from 55°F to 60°F make prime trolling targets, however, since these areas support the preyfish and invertebrates that rainbows feed on. Obviously, a temperature probe that can be lowered into the water column is more useful for locating trout than a surface temperature gauge.

Presentation—Trolling shallow-running baits like spinners and minnowbaits at their normal running depth often is effective during spring and fall. During summer, use deeper-running lures like spoons and plugs, or increase running depth with clip-on weights or three-way rigs. In stained water or when trout are scattered, try trolling baits behind cowbells—a series of small spinner blades on a braided wire leader. Attach a 12- to 24-inch leader to the snap at the terminal end of the cowbell. When trout are wary due to clear water or fishing pressure, try trolling baits behind planer boards. Boards also are effective when trout are feeding on or near the surface. □

Location In Sloping Shorelines

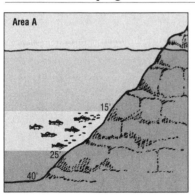
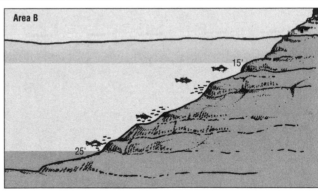

Trout herding minnows near vertical structural Area A tend to be more concentrated than trout feeding over gradual-sloping shorelines like Area B.

Jigging For Brown Trout

STREAM TROUT FEED MORE SELECTIVELY THAN most gamefish. Big trout, though, often feed on bigger items even when small trout are targeting abundant aquatic insects during a hatch. In late fall, winter, and early spring, however, even behemoth stream trout are vulnerable to nymph imitations. Whatever big trout are feeding on, it's important to use a presentation that looks and moves like the real thing. Most of the major forage species in a stream can be imitated by that most versatile of lures, the leadhead jig.

When—

Tackle—*Rod:* 6- to 7-foot light-action spinning rod or 9- to 10-foot fly rod rated for a 5-weight fly-line. *Reel:* lightweight spinning reel with a long-cast spool. *Line:* 2- to 6-pound-test mono.

Rigging—Jigs should be fished near bottom. Switch to slightly heavier jigs as flow velocity increases. Most streams call for 1/32- to 1/16-ounce jigs, but heavier heads offer more control and give trout more time to react.

Presentation—Every stream offers a blend of obstacles. Each obstacle may call for a different retrieve, either across stream, upstream, downstream, or dead vertical. Your approach and cast to a holding area is determined by water clarity, streamside vegetation, and other obstacles, and the path the lure must take to reach the fish. Stay well away from the stream if you're moving, especially when you plan to fish it again on the way back. When dipping a jig vertically into heavy snags and tangles, approach slowly, make no unnecessary movements, and don't disturb the snag.

Jigs imitating nymphs, larvae, and even small minnows catch more trout when presented on a dead drift. Cast across or slightly upstream, keep the line tight, and follow the drift with your rod tip. The jig should tap bottom every 2 to 4 feet. To swim the jig, progressively raise the rod tip as the jig glides downstream. When the rod reaches 1 o'clock, drop the tip as you pick up slack and start over. Sometimes the jig should reach bottom, sometimes it shouldn't, depending on the activity level of the fish. □

Leeches: Lindy Fuzz-E-Grub, Marabou Leech (homemade), McLeod Marabou Leech on a Rat Finkee head, Mister Twister Crappie Jig

Minnows: Northland Gum Drop, Blue Fox Chewee Juice Minnow, Mister Twister Sassy Shiner, and McLeod's Alewife (homemade)

Larvae: Homemade (chenille), Comet Spike, Jack's Jig with Berkley Power Wiggler, McLeod Caddis (poly dubbing—homemade), Northland Gum Drop Head with Berkley Power Grub (water worm larvae)

Crustaceans: Northland Gum Drop, Blue Fox Foxee, plain jig with bass pro Shops Lit'L Squirt, Larew Salt Craw on an Apex Fat Head jig, and Mann's Led Head with Baby Guido Bug

Nymphs: Blue Fox Foxee, homemade marabou, Chewee Juice Nymph, McLeod Articulated Hex (homemade), Mister Twister Grub Bug

Dead Drifts And Swimming Retrieves

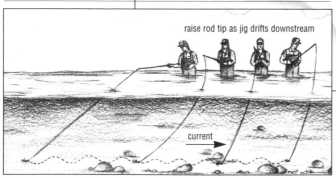

raise rod tip as jig drifts downstream

current

Brown Trout In Winter

DURING WINTER, THE WORLD OF brown trout shrinks. They can't hold in riffles in January. They won't be sucking mayflies from the surface film. They won't hold in the shade of an undercut bank. Even the moderate current found in weed pockets will turn them off. Besides, the terrestrial insects they normally dine on from such lies are absent. Nature slams the door on so many choices that browns are restricted to predictable locations—deep, dark-bottomed holes. These areas absorb heat from the sun and protect fish from predators that can't see into the depths. Areas like these aren't difficult to find, but a subtle and precise presentation is needed to trigger browns in cold water.

When—

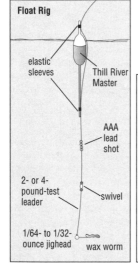

Float Rig

- elastic sleeves
- Thill River Master
- AAA lead shot
- 2- or 4-pound-test leader
- swivel
- 1/64- to 1/32-ounce jighead
- wax worm

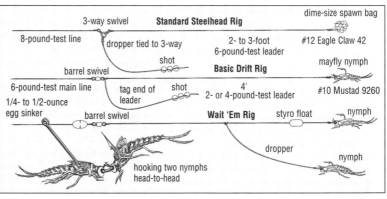

Standard Steelhead Rig

- 3-way swivel
- 8-pound-test line
- dropper tied to 3-way
- shot
- barrel swivel
- 2- to 3-foot 6-pound-test leader
- dime-size spawn bag
- #12 Eagle Claw 42

Basic Drift Rig

- 6-pound-test main line
- 1/4- to 1/2-ounce egg sinker
- tag end of leader
- shot
- 4' 2- or 4-pound-test leader
- mayfly nymph
- #10 Mustad 9260
- barrel swivel

Wait 'Em Rig

- styro float
- nymph
- dropper
- nymph

hooking two nymphs head-to-head

Tackle—*Rod:* 8- to 12-foot medium-power fast-action rod. *Reel:* spinning reel with a long-cast spool. *Line:* 6- or 8-pound-test mono.

Rigging—Be prepared to present baits on drift, set, or float rigs depending on water conditions and fish activity level. Leaders should be long and light—4 feet of 2- to 4-pound test is standard. And hooks need to be sharp, thin, and small to present nymphs naturally in slack water. Slide the point of a #8 or #10 Mustad 9260 or Eagle Claw 80 under the soft shell on the nymph's back.

Presentation—Start at the tail of a hole. Look for current edges. Wade slowly and carefully, but get as close to your casting target as possible without spooking fish. Make a few casts just upstream of your position, drifting the bait along the current edge. Your shot should tap bottom every few feet, moving the rig along at current speed. If it moves too slowly it will snag in rocks or your rig will drag through the sand. If it moves too fast, it won't touch bottom.

Make 4 or 5 casts to each current edge. Your first cast should be the shortest, with each subsequent cast a bit longer. Don't drag a line across a fish 10 feet from you by casting first to the far bank. Note where each cast enters the water. Hook a trout there and you'll want to put your next cast in the same spot. Don't be in a hurry to move upstream. A dozen browns can crowd into an area no bigger than an orange crate. Your task is to find that spot in an acre of water and cast to it from the right position. □

Ideal Wintering Pool

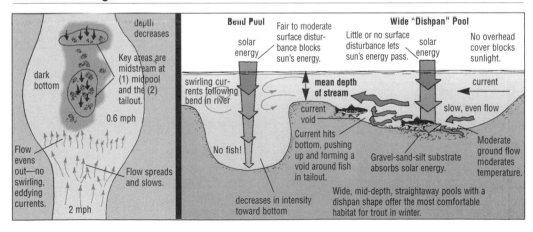

Streamer Strategies For Brook Trout

BROOK TROUT HAVE ALWAYS BEEN A PRIZE CATCH. They're scrappy fighters, excellent table fare, and seemingly eager to attack artificial lures. And while these characteristics endear brook trout to anglers, they also have led to the decline of big fish. A short growing season and small populations mean that even light fishing pressure can quickly crop big brookies from northern rivers. Today, trophy squaretails are confined to a narrow band along the northern extreme of their range. These remote fisheries offer unsurpassed fishing in a beautiful setting, but selective harvest—the practice of keeping a few smaller fish for the table and releasing larger fish—is necessary to sustain quality fishing.

When—

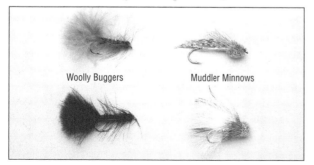

Woolly Buggers   Muddler Minnows

Where— The trophy brook trout band starts in Labrador and extends west through northern Quebec south of the 57th parallel, then south around the tip of James Bay to include Lake Nipigon, then north along Hudson Bay, ending abruptly in the northeast corner of Manitoba.

Tackle— *Rod:* 8- to 9-foot fly rod rated for a #5 to #7 fly line. *Reel:* medium-capacity single-action fly reel. *Line:* #5 to #7 weight-forward fly line and a 9-foot 2X to 4X leader.

Rigging— A couple of basic streamer patterns will take big squaretails anywhere they swim. The muddler minnow was designed by Don Gapen to fool the brookies of northern Ontario, and it remains one of the most versatile and effective flies available. Carry weighted and unweighted versions tied on #2 to #8 hooks to

Casting Flies

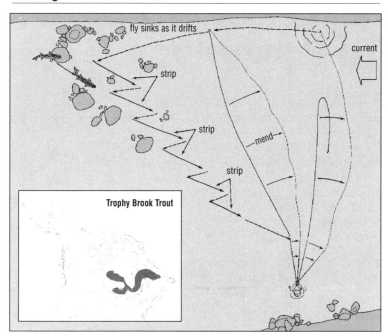

Trophy Brook Trout

match available forage. Whether brook trout see the Woolly Bugger as a baitfish or a large nymph is unclear, but they attack this simple pattern with abandon. Carry an assortment of sizes in natural and fluorescent colors.

Presentation— Make your first cast across stream, then begin quartering downstream. Start with short casts and put a little more line into each succeeding throw. After covering the far

bank or reaching maximum distance, move downstream a few feet and begin again. As the line is about to straighten on the cast, throw the rod tip upstream slightly, throwing a curve of line above the fly. This allows the fly to sink longer before current forms a bow in the line and drags the fly. When the fly does drag, mend line by rolling the rod over in an upstream arc. When the fly begins to swing across the current at the tail of the pool, retrieve the line in short jerks. □

A Versatile Approach To Brook Trout

B ROOK TROUT IN STREAMS ADAPT TO A constantly changing environment. High water and fast current pushes brookies behind obstructions, while low water forces them into the safety of deep pools. Aggressive fish may move into food-rich riffles, but fish in a negative feeding mood often sulk beneath undercut banks. When they're feeding, they may target emerging insects on the surface, nymphs on the bottom, or baitfish anywhere in between. To catch these fish consistently, match your rigs and presentations to the conditions.

When—

Floats

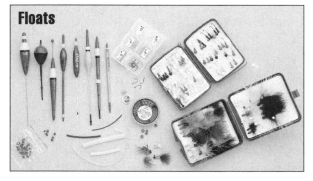

Floats are the ultimate barrier beater. If you can't stand in the perfect spot to fish a stream segment, use a float to deliver livebaits, jigs, plastics, even hardware, several hundred feet downstream. More importantly, floats present bait or flies naturally. The bait moves at current speed into areas where trout can't see, feel, or even hear you—critical in low water on ultra-clear streams. To match various current speeds, carry a selection of fixed and slip floats, and lead shot to balance floats.

Tackle—*Rod:* 6- to 8-foot light-power spinning rod. *Reel:* medium-capacity spinning reel. *Line:* 4- to 8-pound-test mono, depending on cover.

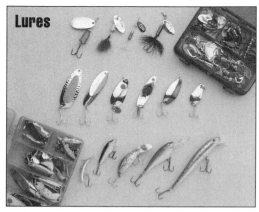

Lures

Lures cover water. If you don't know a stream, the first thing out of your vest might be a spinner, spoon, or minnowbait. Choose hardware sizes that match the flow. Determine this by casting cross-stream and letting the lure drift. Don't retrieve until it's straight downstream. If the lure bangs or drags bottom, it's too heavy. If it ticks bottom occasionally, it's just right. Once you know a stream, weight your selection toward that size.

Flies

Flies are the most versatile tools in your vest. They imitate aquatic insects, terrestrial insects, and minnows—tho throo major food groups of trout. Match what lives in the stream you fish. Imitate size, shape, and color. In conjunction with spinning tackle, a clear plastic casting bubble allows presentation of flies.

Terminal Tackle

Many days, these will be the only tools needed. Learning to drift livebait naturally along bottom is the basis to mastering other trout techniques. Carry a selection of lead shot to match current speed, and #14 to #4 light-wire hooks to match the size of the bait. Color may also make a difference—try larger gold hooks in cloudy water, smaller bronze hooks in clear water.

Run 'N Gun Spinner Techniques For Steelhead

THE STRAIGHT SHAFT SPINNER IS AN awesome fish-catching lure. Most game-fish at one time or another will jump on the right size spinner presented in the right way. Steelhead are no exception. Why do they strike spinners? Territorial aggression, perhaps. Anger. Curiosity. Reflex. All theories. Fact is, steelhead slam spinners in every season of the year and in just about any condition imaginable. They take them out West as well as in tributaries of the Great Lakes.

When—

Tackle— *Rod:* 6½- to 7½-foot fast-action spinning rod. *Reel:* spinning reel with a long-cast spool and a smooth drag. *Line:* 8- to 17-pound-test abrasion-resistant mono.

Presentation— Covering a long-bend pool in a medium-size stream when fish are on the bite takes about 15 casts. Start on the down-stream end to avoid kicking silt over fish you haven't discovered. Steelhead face upstream. Approach them from the tail so they spot the spinner before they spot you.

Position A—Cover the tailout with progressively longer casts. Move up and rifle three casts tight to the submerged deadfall, using a quick drop to get down fast.

Position B—Use a sweep cast leading the spinner with the rod, to get under the fallen tree. Keep the rod tip low and let the lure work its way out.

Position C—Snags or no snags, stop at the

middle of the pool and cover water. Three casts, tops.

Position D— Always punch a few casts on the hoof between stopping points. In this case, work the spinner along the upstream face of the logjam.

Position E— Probe the head of the pool, a classic lie for active steelhead, with several casts. Combine the sweep with the quick drop by raising the rod as the spinner nears the lip of the hole. Head for the next pool, dropping a cast into every marginal holding area along the way. □

The Sweep Cast

Cast straight across stream, letting the current work the blade. The crucial moment occurs at the end of the swing— the spinner turns, crosses the stream, and rises. Hang on!

The Quick-Drop

Cast the spinner at an upstream angle, then close the bail and raise the rod (Position 1). Keep the rod high and the line fairly tight while the spinner drops toward the bottom (Position 2). When the spinner taps bottom, lower the rod, and let the spinner sweep through the hole (Position 3).

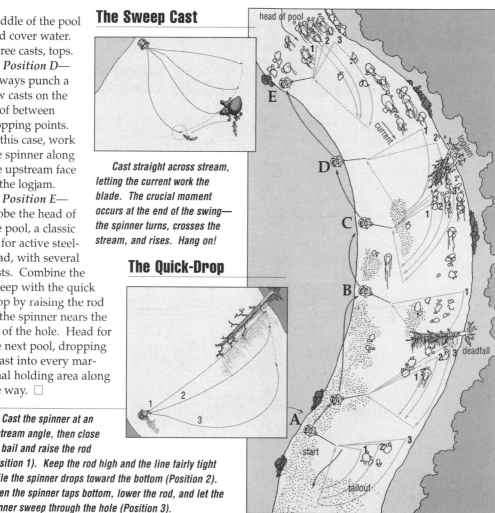

Simple Is Better For Steelhead In Woods

THE BASIC LEAD SHOT DRIFT rig can be used for any predatory fish in moving water, but it's particularly good for steelhead in wood-filled streams. Components include lead shot and a hook. Add a swivel or portion of lighter leader material to fine-tune your presentation, but that's usually not necessary. Cast this rig with confidence into heavy cover and bring it back out again. It's amazingly snag-resistant, but if you do get hung up you're only out a nickel's worth of tackle and a single knot.

When—

Tackle— *Rod:* 8- to 10-foot fast-action spinning rod. *Reel:* spinning reel with a large-diameter spool and a smooth drag. *Line:* 6- to 8-pound-test abrasion-resistant mono.

Rigging— In heavy wood cover, the hook is the component that snags most often. Hooks with straight points hit submerged timber and stick like darts. Beaked hooks (those with curved in tips) often deflect off wood, eliminating several frustrating hang-ups per day. Thin-wire models like the Mustad 9260D often can be straightened with a steady pull. Bend it back into shape with a pliers and it's again ready to hook and land fish.

Lead shot should be pinched lightly enough to not damage line, but tightly enough to stay in place when a steelhead drags the rig through the water at 20 mph. When breakoffs occur, the hook usually is the only component lost. Slide the shot up the line, cut off any abraded leader, and tie on another hook. Eared shot is easier to remove to match changing depth and current velocity, but round shot drifts better. European-style double-cut shot combines the best attributes of both—drifts true in current yet is easy to remove.

Shot placement also can reduce snags. Near dense wood tangles, use a short 6- to 12-inch leader to drift the bait under the cover. Longer leaders tend to flail in current and wrap around

branches. For logs lying across the bottom, however, use a leader up to 3 feet long to keep the hook riding above the snag. Styrofoam float beads added to a spawn bag give the hook additional buoyancy. □

Shot Rigs

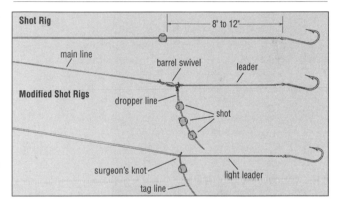

Shot Placement Improves Snag Resistance

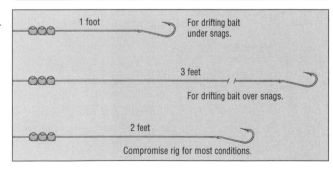

Ice-Fishing For Lake Trout

DURING SUMMER, LAKE TROUT ARE forced into the deep cold water below the thermocline. They may inhabit deep water during winter, too, but they also roam shallow flats where few anglers look for them. Fishing shallower water is more efficient, too—you can fish more efficiently in 40 feet of water than in 80 feet, and you can use lighter baits and still get to the bottom faster. And while most lake trout fishermen are content to sit over a single hole for days, a mobile approach produces more and bigger fish in less time. Fishing fast in areas other anglers overlook is the key to consistent lake trout action on ice.

When—

Tackle— *Rod:* 3- to 4-foot medium-power ice rod. *Reel:* medium-capacity casting or spinning reel. *Line:* 8- to 12-pound-test mono.

Rigging— Since you'll be fishing in water about 20 to 80 feet deep, lures that sink fast are most efficient. Begin with a large swimming lure—something like a 3/8-ounce Northland Air-Plane Jig or a 3/8-ounce System Tackle Walleye Flyer tipped with a 4-inch shiner. If you see fish move in on your sonar but they don't take, try a 1/4-ounce swimming jig dressed with a 3-inch tube body and tipped with a piece of minnow. For finicky lakers, try a 4-inch livebait anchored by a 1/4- or 3/8-ounce plain leadhead jig.

Location—Shallow bays on lake arms aren't lake trout water. Instead, look for trout in deep main-lake sections. But relatively shallow water is still important for locating concentrations of fish. Not just any shallow water, but shallower structural elements in the deep portion of the lake. Points like *Area A*, saddle areas between islands like *Area B*, humps like *Area C*, and saddle areas between points like *Area D* all are potential trout attractors. When trout are over a flat surface or gradual slope, they often feed right on the bottom. If the fish are holding along the quick-dropping edge, however, they tend to suspend over deep water.

Presentation—Let your jig fall to the bottom under light tension. Bites often occur on the drop, so keep the line fairly tight on the way down. Once the jig hits bottom, lift it off the bottom and slowly pump it up and down a few times. Reel up 5 feet or so and repeat the process. Until a depth pattern develops, fish this method all the way

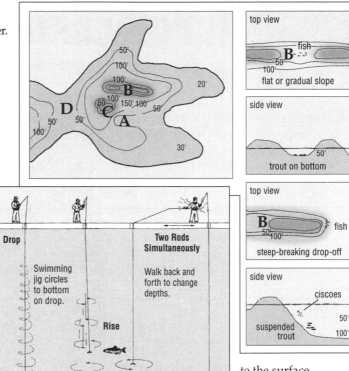

to the surface.

Where two rods are legal, fish two holes about 20 feet apart. Drop one jig to the bottom and the other about halfway down. Walk back and forth between holes with a rod in each hand. As you move toward one hole, that jig drops while the other rises. □

Trolling For Lake Trout

T HE KEY TO CATCHING TROPHY LAKE trout is understanding seasonal fish location. When trout inhabit shallow water in spring and fall, they're easy targets for walleye and pike anglers armed with traditional spinning and casting tackle. When they move deep in summer, however, you need the right gear. Catching these fish requires a presentation system that puts lures in front of fish in 80 to 120 feet of water. Even on popular Canadian trophy fisheries, fish residing in water deeper than 50 feet often remain an untapped resource.

When—

Tackle—

Rod: 7½-foot flippin' stick. *Reel:* large-capacity baitcasting reel. *Line:* 20- to 30-pound-test

stranded or solid stainless steel wire for the main line and a 14- to 20-pound-test mono leader.

Rigging— Big spoons and lures can be presented effectively in deep water on three-way rigs, and the length of the monofilament dropper line can be adjusted to the level of the fish. A one-foot dropper is used for bottom-oriented fish, while an 8-foot dropper may be necessary for fish holding off the bottom. Depending on the depth of water, lure, and trolling speed, 4 to 8 ounces of weight may be needed to maintain bottom contact. The

James Lindner's Trophy Lake Trout Rig

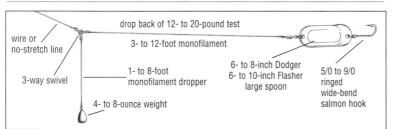

wire or no-stretch line

3-way swivel

drop back of 12- to 20-pound test

3- to 12-foot monofilament

1- to 8-foot monofilament dropper

4- to 8-ounce weight

6- to 8-inch Dodger
6- to 10-inch Flasher
large spoon

5/0 to 9/0 ringed wide-bend salmon hook

length of the leader varies from 3 to 12 feet, with 4 to 8 feet most common. Shorter leaders create an erratic lure action that often triggers aggressive fish. Longer leaders allow a more subtle presentation for less aggressive lakers.

Large spoons and crankbaits from 6 to 16 inches long attract trophy trout. Big lakers are attracted to large flutter spoons, but no lure manufacturer makes a 10-inch spoon. Make your own flutter spoon by attaching salmon-style hooks to a 6- to 8-inch Luhr-Jensen Dodger or a 6- to 10-inch Abe 'N Al Flasher. Properly tuned and trolled at the right speed, this lure wobbles and flashes with a controlled side-to-side swaying action that triggers big fish. Bend the lure slightly to achieve the appropriate action.

Large spoons, dodgers, and flashers—*homemade 16-inch spoon, Luhr-Jensen 00 Dodger, Abe 'N Al 001 Flasher, Abe 'N Al 0087 Flasher, Luhr-Jensen O Dodger.* Crankbaits—*Normark Rapala Magnum CD 26, Arbogast AC Plug, The Believer.* Spoons and blades—*Eppinger Muskie-Devle Spoon, Eppinger Red Eye Spoon (2½-ounce), Magnum Blitz Blade.* Jigs with plastics—*Kalin's Grub (10 inches), Blakemore Road Runner (1 ounce), Jack's Shad (9 inches).*

Presentation—Run lures next to the boat to determines how they respond at various speeds. A lure that darts forward, stalls, then flutters down consistently triggers trophy trout. Once you're moving at the proper speed, hit the freespool button and lower the rig to the bottom. For maximum control, maintain a 30- to 45-degree angle on your line as it works through typical 80- to 120-foot depths. Pump the rod occasionally to vary lure action. Lift and drop the sinker to thump bottom and maintain contact while trolling. When depth changes, take up slack as you move shallower or release line as you move deeper. When you see suspended fish on sonar, reel the lure up to the fish. □

Spoon Feeding Arctic Char

S EA-RUN ARCTIC CHAR ARE FOUND farther north than any other fish in North American freshwater, but the ice-cold water has little effect on the strength and endurance of these powerful fish. Small fish may jump several times when hooked, but big char just keep pulling until you stop them or your reel is stripped of line. They're also less wary than other salmonids. Arctic char fresh from the sea often strike the first several lures that cross their path, even after being caught and released several times. As for table quality, many consider the char's orange flesh superior in flavor and texture to the finest salmon.

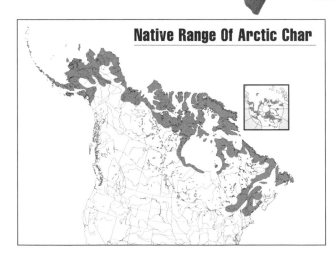

Native Range Of Arctic Char

When—

Tackle— *Rod:* 7- to 9-foot medium-heavy-power spinning rod. *Reel:* large-capacity spinning reel. *Line:* 12- to 20-pound-test abrasion-resistant mono.

Where—Arctic char are circumpolar. The European Arctic char is found from the British Isles through Scandinavia and into Russia, where another subspecies ranges to the Bering Sea. During a colder period from 7,000 to 15,000 years ago, Arctic char roamed farther south and farther inland. Relicts of these forays remain trapped deep in ancient oligotrophic lakes of northeastern North America. The blueback trout of Maine, the redback trout of Quebec, the Sunapee golden trout of New Hampshire, and other forms found in New Brunswick remain classified as North American Arctic char.

Rigging—Techniques for catching char are no different from those used for trout and salmon. In shallow or running water they readily take a fly. Bait (especially minnows and salmon eggs), spinners, and crankbaits also are effective. But of all the Arctic char caught each year, probably 80 percent or more are taken with spoons. From August through October, anglers position themselves at the mouth or along the banks of spawning streams. Use thick casting spoons to get down in current and to cast long distances across huge northern rivers. The best spoon is one that matches the current flow, drifting naturally just off bottom over the longest stretch.

Presentation—Spoons can be retrieved several ways to catch Arctic char. The most effective method is to follow the lure's movement with your rod tip so it barely touches bottom or hovers just above bottom throughout the drift. Whether you snag, tap, or stay off bottom completely can be controlled by rod position. The trajectory of the lure when the rod is held high (Cast A) is short. It hits bottom quickly because the current drags less line. The same lure taps bottom occasionally when the rod is held at half mast (Cast B). The longest drift is achieved when the rod is held low (Cast C), parallel to the water, and the rod tip leads the lure. □

Drifting Spoons

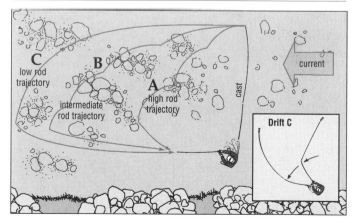

Fishing For Dolly Varden & Bull Trout

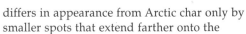

Joe Tomelleri

MISUNDERSTOOD AND maligned for over a century, Dolly Varden and their kin the bull trout have suffered many indignities. Bounties and unlimited legal harvest reveal a history of low esteem by anglers and fisheries managers. Considered a voracious predator of more highly valued trout species, in Alaska during the first half of the century a bounty of 2½ cents was offered for the head of each Dolly. Up to $20,000 per year was spent on such bounties during the 1930s. But Dolly Varden and bull trout may be gaining respect with today's fishermen and fisheries mangers. The days of bounties, at least, are almost over.

Dolly Varden— The
Dolly Varden, which ranges from Japan north through Kamchatka, into Alaska and south to Puget Sound, often differs in appearance from Arctic char only by smaller spots that extend farther onto the back. But freshwater Dollies in some environments may also closely resemble another char, the brook trout. The wormlike vermiculations along the back of the Dolly are either absent or faint, and the tail of the Dolly has a more distinct fork. The anadromous form of Dolly Varden is silver at sea.

Dolly Varden spawn in October and November, but may enter streams early to take advantage of the free-drifting Pacific salmon eggs. Slip a plastic egg the size of a salmon egg on a length of mono leader and peg it above a single hook with a doubled piece of rubber band. Tie the leader to a barrel swivel and attach enough lead shot to the tag end of the leader knot to keep the rig bouncing along the bottom in current. On some Alaskan streams, it's not unusual to catch a hundred Dollys per day by drifting this rig behind spawning king, sockeye, or pink salmon.

Bull Trout— Bull trout, depending on region, often resemble either lake trout or Dolly Varden. Their backs are generally gray or light olive green, and their spots are smaller, rounder, and often more colorful than those of lake trout, ranging from cream to pale yellow or pink. The tail is less forked than a laker's, and the jaw usually doesn't extend past the eye. The strongest population exists in the Metolius River drainage of central Oregon, where it's now protected from harvest.

Like lake trout, bull trout in lakes spend most of the year in deep cold water. They also fall to the same presentation—trolling large spoons on leadcore lines and long mono leaders. But when lake trout are introduced into native bull trout waters, bull trout often are unable to compete and their population dwindles. Fishing for this fragile species should not be taken lightly. Check regulations or ask biologists about the status of local populations. □

Native Range Of Dolly Varden

Native Range Of Bull Trout

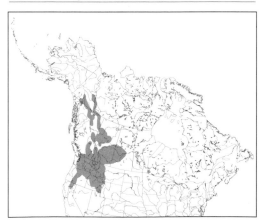

Finding And Catching Kokanee Salmon

I N SOME ENVIRONMENTS THEY AVERAGE A FOOT or less in length, yet "ferocity beyond belief" describes the attitude of the smallest salmon, the kokanee. They will maul lures half their own length, which is strange behavior for any fish, but downright weird for a plankton eater. Like ferocious little dogs that always bark and growl, kokanees apparently feel they have to prove something. Fortunate for those who pursue them, since the bright red flesh of the kokanee is the finest table fare from freshwater.

Native Range Of The Kokanee Salmon

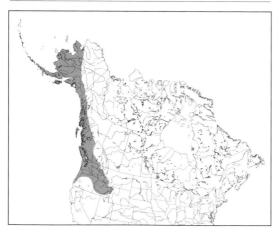

When—

Tackle—*Rod:* 6- to 8-foot light-power trolling or spinning rod. *Reel:* medium-capacity baitcasting or spinning reel. *Line:* 4- to 8-pound-test mono.

Location— Kokanee are a cold-water fish, preferring water temperatures from 50 °F to 59 °F, though they can tolerate temperatures of 65 °F. Temperatures above 74 °F become lethal. In spring, kokanee often inhabit the top 10 feet of the water column—in shallow bays with frequent insect hatches, or over deep water. As surface temperatures warm in summer, kokanee move deeper. Temperature fluctuations, like upwellings, bring kokanee inshore briefly, and extensive daily vertical movements are common. Kokanee are drawn to upwellings, which gather plankton along the edge of masses of water with different temperatures and densities.

fly-fishing approach to spring and fall. Look for rising fish early in the morning or late in the evening when insects are coming off the water.

When surface waters warm in bays, kokanee move to the main lake. As surface waters in the main lake warm in summer, the fish move deeper, but like ciscoes, they often rise to within 20 or 30 feet of the surface to feed during low-light periods and can be triggered by surprisingly aggressive trolling techniques. Put a #1 or #2 straight-shaft spinner on an 18-inch leader behind a cowbell attractor, and troll at 1½ to 3 mph along temperature breaks or through known feeding areas. □

Presentation—
During the spawning run in rivers and streams, kokanee may be caught on egg-imitating flies, beads, or plastic eggs, but spring and summer are the best times to catch them. When hatches of lake-dwelling mayfly nymphs and midge pupae swarm to the surface from the bottom of mid-depth bays, kokanee can be taken on flies. The key is finding an insect hatch in water below 60 °F, which often confines the

Kokanee Rig

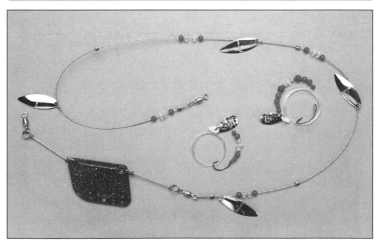

Finding And Catching Arctic Grayling

NATIVES OF THE CANADIAN SHIELD HAVE been harvesting Arctic grayling for centuries—sometimes to feed themselves, but more often to feed their dogs. While the delicate flavor of grayling may pale in comparison to whitefish and lake trout, their sporting attributes do not. Grayling are abundant in many waters, easy to catch on a variety of natural and artificial baits, and often jump when hooked. They also are beautiful to behold—their sail-like dorsal fin and striking purple, blue, and pink coloration make them one of the most sought after trophies of the North.

When—

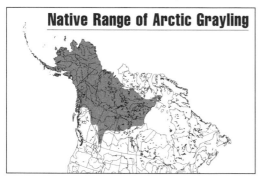

Native Range of Arctic Grayling

Tackle— *Rod:* 6- to 7-foot light-power spinning rod or 5-weight fly rod. *Reel:* medium-capacity spinning reel or single-action fly reel. *Line:* 4- or 6-pound-test mono, or 5-weight weight-forward floating fly line.

Rigging— Arctic grayling feed primarily on insects, making them a popular quarry for fly-fishermen. Dry flies and nymph imitations that match the size and color of observed aquatic and terrestrial insects are most effective, though grayling rarely refuse any well-presented pattern. Medium-size streamer patterns, particularly those that imitate sculpins, are a good choice for trophy grayling. Spoons and spinners should be matched to water depth and current speed—1/16-ounce lures usually suffice in shallow riffles, but 1/8-ounce baits often are necessary for probing deep pools. When other salmonids are spawning, natural and imitation salmon eggs also are a good bait.

Location— The native range of the Arctic grayling extends from the Canadian Shield west to Siberia and south to the headwaters of the Missouri River. They thrive in the coldest clearest waters this region has to offer—from small rocky streams to swift rivers to deep infertile lakes. In streams, grayling often form large schools in deep pools and behind current breaks. The largest members of the school usually are positioned at the forward edge of the break, allowing anglers to selectively target trophy fish. In lakes, grayling usually inhabit the top 10 feet of the water column, but may suspend over much deeper water. The best time to find and catch grayling in lakes is during an insect hatch, when they rise to sip emerging insects from the surface.

Presentation—Casting dry flies is the most effective way to catch surface-feeding

Current Strategies

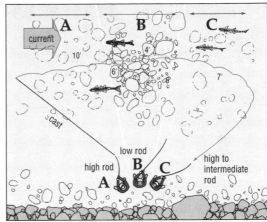

grayling, but hardware shines for bottom-holding fish. While fly-fishermen mend their line in current to eliminate drag, most spin fishermen just cast and retrieve. Cover more productive water with fewer casts by matching rod position to varying depths and current speeds. To fish the hole, the ridge in front, and the depression behind requires several rod positions. Cast upstream (*A*) and hold your rod high to reduce the effect of the current. Approaching the ridge (*B*), drop your rod downstream and parallel to the water. This allows the current to bow the line and pull the lure up. As the rig crests the ridge and drops into the subsequent pool (*C*), raise your rod again to minimize drag and allow the lure to drop into deeper water. □

Splake Through The Seasons

THE NAME SPLAKE BORROWS "SP" from the specked trout, the common name for the brook trout in New York and Ontario, and "lake" from lake trout, the female parent of this hybrid. The splake's value as a gamefish and popularity with anglers stems first from its fast growth. Splake stocked in Lake Huron reached 15 pounds in less than 6 years. And with two rather gullible fish species as parents, splake often are eager biters. This accommodating nature is also due to the splake's omnivorous diet, which may in turn be due to a scarcity of prey in many infertile lakes. They're also as tasty as any fish in freshwater—broiled, baked, or panfried. These characteristics coupled with a distribution across 11 northern states and several Canadian provinces have made splake a year-round favorite with anglers.

Splake tend to be most active and catchable in the spring, but they're also spread out. Keep moving between high-percentage locations to locate a concentration of fish. Splake often cluster near the mouths of tributary streams or on gravel shoals where suckers spawn, feeding on

Mann's Winger

their eggs. At the same time, a group of fish may be feeding offshore, foraging on emerging insects. Troll a small spinner tipped with a dead minnow until you find fish, then anchor and cast.

Once the surface temperature of the lake warms into the low 60°F range, splake move down to or below the thermocline. In infertile lakes, the deepest layer of water supports enough oxygen to support splake. Vertical jigging or downrigging spinners, spoons, or flies are proven presentations, yet few anglers pursue these fish in summer. Three-way rigs presented on wire line also are effective for fish holding in water deeper than 40 feet.

Reef Runner Slender Spoon

When splake begin to gather near spawning reefs, it's possible to catch dozens in an afternoon. Male splake are dressed in their vibrant spawning colors—bright red bellies and the white-edged fins characteristic of brook trout. Trolling or casting spoons and spinners along the edges of spawning reefs is effective. If fish seem spooky or unwilling to pursue a fast-moving lure, try drifting a dead minnow suspended beneath a slip float.

Splake thrive in the cold water of winter, often biting aggressively. They often are caught on large swimming jigs and spoons targeted for lake trout, but splake anglers usually begin with a 1/4-ounce jigging spoon tipped with a piece of minnow. Cut a series of holes along the edge of a drop off and watch for fish on sonar. Splake typically cruise two to five feet off the bottom, and baits presented just above this level attract the most fish. □

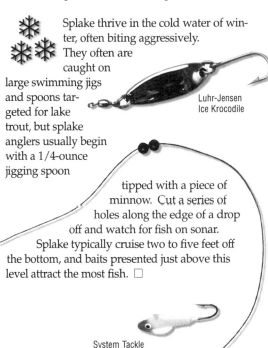
Luhr-Jensen Ice Krocodile

Deadbait Rig

System Tackle Walleye Flyer

Deadbait Tactics For Pike

SPRING IS PRIME TIME FOR PIKE. THE BIGGEST FISH in the lake are concentrated in shallow marshy bays and the fishing is supposed to be easy. But what if it's not? If big pike are around but won't hit spoons, spinnerbaits, straight-shaft spinners, jigs, or large flies, flip-flop and try motionless or near-motionless tactics. Big pike commonly eat dead minnows, suckers, smelt, and small gamefish, especially during winter and cold-water periods when baitfish don't decompose. Lunker pike scavenge dead fish off the bottom, reacting more like aquatic vacuum cleaners than savage predators. Put a deadbait in front of them and you'll catch them under the toughest conditions.

Pike Location

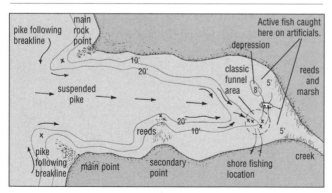

When—

Tackle— *Rod:* 7½-foot flippin' stick. *Reel:* medium-capacity baitcasting reel. *Line:* 12- or 14-pound-test mono.

Rigging— Light-wire deadbait rigs are subtle and efficient. Two #6 trebles should be positioned 2 to 4 inches apart, with the end hook inserted below the bait's dorsal fin and the lead hook near the tail. In dark water, fish bait on or near the bottom. In clear water, insert a slip float or a piece of balsa wood into the bait's gullet to suspend it where the fish more easily can see it. Fresh-killed, frozen, or preserved baitfish are all effective baits.

Location— In early spring, the back ends of marshy bays, weedy river inlets, or reservoir coves tend to attract pike. Many linger in the general area after spawning, unless the water warms too quickly to uncomfortable levels. These areas become prime feeding grounds where minnows and other baitfish gather to feed or spawn. Forage that dies in the area rests on the bottom, providing an easy food source when pike aren't seeking live targets.

Presentation— Don't use deadbaits to cover a lot of water; they work best at rest or barely moving. Set up in funnels or key locations that draw fish to you, rather than attempting to fish large areas to locate fish. Position your boat so you

can cast two deadbait lines in the funnel area and a third in a depression that may draw fish during off-peak conditions. Use another line to fancast spoons to the shallows and draw pike toward the deadbaits. Cover key features of prime bays and the pike will come. □

Deadbait Rigs

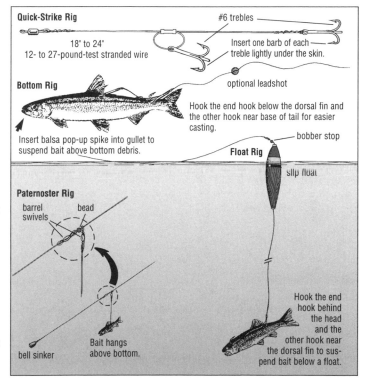

Quick-Strike Rig

18" to 24"
12- to 27-pound-test stranded wire

#6 trebles

Insert one barb of each treble lightly under the skin.

optional leadshot

Bottom Rig

Insert balsa pop-up spike into gullet to suspend bait above bottom debris.

Hook the end hook below the dorsal fin and the other hook near base of tail for easier casting.

bobber stop

Float Rig

slip float

Paternoster Rig

barrel swivels   bead

bell sinker   Bait hangs above bottom.

Hook the end hook behind the head and the other hook near the dorsal fin to suspend bait below a float.

A Mobile Approach For Ice Pike

BIG PIKE ARE AVAILABLE TO MORE anglers through the ice than during the open-water season. In most areas, pike aren't being targeted. In reservoirs in the Dakotas and across the Mountain West; in lakes in Iowa and Minnesota; in backwaters off the Mississippi River; and in many bays of the Great Lakes, panfish and walleyes are being fished for, but not so often pike. In areas where anglers do set up for pike, most of them plant a shack in a bay at first-ice and stay there for the rest of the season. This fishing demands mobility. Granted, tip-ups key fishing for pike. But tip-ups don't have to be a totally stationary presentation; that is, in most situations, they shouldn't be set in the same spot for more than a few hours.

When—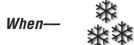

Quick-Strike Rigs

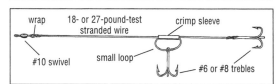

wrap | 18- or 27-pound-test stranded wire | crimp sleeve
#10 swivel | small loop | #6 or #8 trebles

Tackle— *Tip-ups:* stationary or wind tip-ups. *Line:* 36-pound-test dacron or teflon-coated ice line.

Rigging— Use quick-strike rigs consisting of two #6 or #8 trebles rigged in tandem on 12- to 27-pound-test stranded wire. The distance

Depth Zones For Tip-Ups

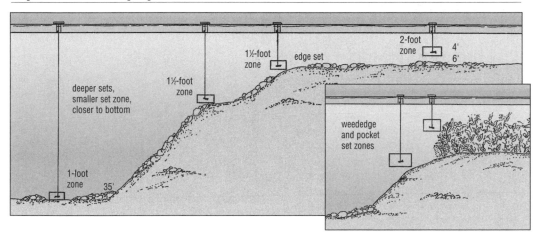

between the hooks depends on the size of the bait. As good as deadbait can be for pike, live-bait often attracts more fish. Use the liveliest 5- or 6-inch shiners or chubs you can find. Hook baitfish so they swim down and away from the rigging—the end treble behind the head and the top treble near the dorsal fin.

Location— Typical habitat areas in lakes include weededges in bays, particularly points and pockets in the edge; main-lake flats or bars with weedgrowth; and occasionally, rocky points, especially points that are part of a sunken island near classic shallow weedy habitat. In river backwaters, probe along weededges, the edges of the deepest holes in the backwater, and where current runs adjacent to

the opening of the backwater. In reservoirs, try flats and channel cuts in the back end of creek arms; then work your way back out of the arm, checking each point along the way.

Presentation— On a typical spot, set several tip-ups in various areas that pike prowl— along the deep edge of points or in pockets in a weededge, and in open pockets on the weed flat. On rocky areas, set tip-ups on the rock flat near the drop along the crest of the main drop-off, and at the base of the drop-off. In small areas, give pike an hour to respond. In larger areas, give them two hours. If pike don't bite within this time, or if the action stops, don't wait for a change in their aggressiveness. Move to another area. □

Short-Lining For Shallow Pike

THE PRACTICE OF CANE-POLE trolling (or short-line poling) with lures is over 100 years old. Most practitioners have traded in their cane poles for long rods and reels and their oars for outboards, but the basic technique remains unchanged. Sounds primitive, but this ancient art has its strong points. With long rods and short lines, sensitivity is

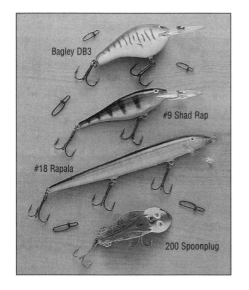

Bagley DB3

#9 Shad Rap

#18 Rapala

200 Spoonplug

acute. Swing lures in, check for weeds, and swing them back out. Move the rod tip to guide lures over or around visible weeds or into pockets and cuts. Precise control and efficient coverage make this system one of the best options going for pike in shallow water.

When—

Tackle— *Rod:* 10- to 15-foot heavy-action spinning or casting rod. *Reel:* medium-capacity spinning or casting reel with a smooth drag. *Line:* 17- or 20-pound-test abrasion-resistant mono.

Rigging— What makes this system different from other trolling methods is the amount of line between you and your lure. Line length from the tip of the rod to the lure should be the same as the rod length. This offers maximum control over the running depth and placement of the lure. Spoons and spinners are traditional favorites, but deep-diving crankbaits and shallow-running minnowbaits also are effective. And while wire leaders prevent bite-offs, some short-line trollers don't bother. They opt instead for a Cross-Lok snap, claiming the increased number of strikes more than makes up for the few fish they lose each season.

Presentation— Short-line poling for pike isn't a highly technical art, but attention to detail keeps things running smoothly and allows efficient coverage. An angler in the front of the boat can run a rod the same length as the boat driver, but a longer rod affords longer range. The rear angler already has one hand occupied, so a shorter rod makes sense. And he's going to keep himself a comfortable rod's length from the weedline, so the front angler should be able to adjust for a longer or shorter reach.

One lure should run near the base of the weed wall, a foot or so off bottom. Deep-running crankbaits like the Bagley DB3 or the 200 Spoonplug are a good choice. The other lure should run just over the deepest weeds, or higher than the other lure against the edge. Try a one-ounce Rubbercor sinker ahead of a #18 Floating Rapala. Pike cruising outside the weededge part to either side of the boat. If they've been relating to weeds, chances are they'll head in that direction, placing them in the path of the lures. □

Pole Coverage

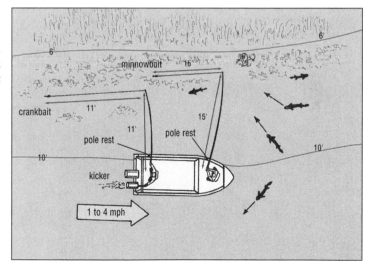

Speed Trolling For Pike

ONCE SUMMER SETS IN, THE OUTSIDE weedline is the focal point for pike activity in most natural lakes and reservoirs. In clear lakes, the deep edge of the weedline may run 12 to 17 or even 20 feet deep, the average being 10 to 15 feet. And in murky lakes, it may be as shallow as 4 to 7 feet. Points and inside turns in the outside weed-edge on major main-lake bars usually attract pike, mainly because these areas are passing or gathering points for baitfish—perch, bull-heads, ciscoes, suckers, or small gamefish, depending on the body of water.

When—

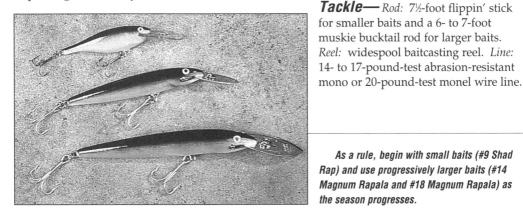

Tackle— *Rod:* 7½-foot flippin' stick for smaller baits and a 6- to 7-foot muskie bucktail rod for larger baits. *Reel:* widespool baitcasting reel. *Line:* 14- to 17-pound-test abrasion-resistant mono or 20-pound-test monel wire line.

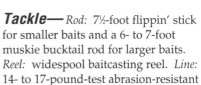

As a rule, begin with small baits (#9 Shad Rap) and use progressively larger baits (#14 Magnum Rapala and #18 Magnum Rapala) as the season progresses.

Rigging—If you don't use wire line, you need a wire leader. Buy leaders with a Cross-Lok snap on the terminal end and a good swivel on the other end, or make your own from 27-pound-test single-strand wire.

Presentation—Run crankbaits behind a boat moving forward at 3 to 7 mph just outside the edge of the weeds. With two fishermen each using one rod, run one lure about mid-depth, the other a foot or two off the bottom. Pike have an ultrasensitive lateral line system that lets them feel baits long before they see them. Different types of plugs give off different vibration patterns. As a rule, tighter patterns caused by a faster vibration work best during early summer. Wider patterns become more productive as summer progresses.

Consider using wire line to get deeper faster and work more efficiently through the edge of weeds. When your lure contacts weeds, rip your rod tip forward to snap the lure through the edge. If weeds hang on the bait, rip several more times to snap them off. The rip also serves as a triggering maneuver. Constantly pump your rod tip forward a foot or two. Then stop and the let the rod tip drift back to its starting position. The lure hustles forward, changing its wobble as it goes, then slows and limps along. Following pike often can't resistance the sudden change in action. □

Trolling Weed Edges

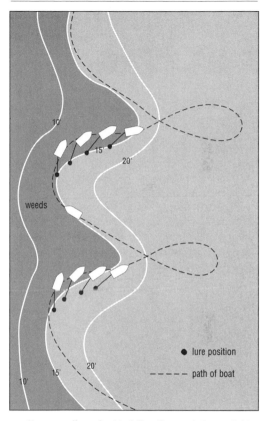

Keep your lines short to follow the weededge as tight as possible. As you approach a turn, let the boat move over the weeds for a short distance, then slowly move back to deeper water. Make an outside turn on points to keep lures on track.

Spin Rigs For Pike

SUCCESSFUL GUIDES, THOSE WITH clothed wives and well-fed children, often have a bait or two they reserve for the toughest conditions—a lure that produces fish and income during the doggiest days of summer. The Lindy Spin Rig was such a weapon. The simplicity and productivity of the rig almost guaranteed pike for skilled and unskilled clients alike. Just hook a big minnow through the lips, cast it out, and catch pike all afternoon. While the Spin Rig is no longer made, the Gopher Bait Spin, a variety of skirtless short-arm spinner-bait, or a homemade rig of similar design still produces pike.

When—

Tackle— *Rod:* 6½- to 7½-foot medium-heavy-power casting or spinning rod. *Reel:* medium-capacity baitcasting or spinning reel. *Line:* 12- or 14-pound-test mono.

Rigging— It's not unusual to tie directly to a spin rig with monofilament and fish for several days without getting bitten off, then suddenly be

Use lively minnows ranging from 3½ to 5½ inches. Shiners and creek chubs are favored, but suckers and other minnows also work well. For casting or trolling, insert the hook into the minnow's mouth and out through the middle of the head.

cut off by the next half dozen fish. Depends on the size of the fish and how they strike the bait. The problem with these lures is the open line-tie loop. The snap at the terminal end of a commercial wire leader often slides up the arm of the bait.

Make your own leaders from 18- or 27-pound-test noncoated stranded wire. Cut a piece about 14 inches long. Wrap the wire twice through a small swivel, leaving a 1-inch tag. Lock a forceps on the end of the tag. Now, holding the swivel with one hand and the leader with the other, swing the forceps forward around the leader. Repeat the process to secure the bait to the wire.

Combo Casting And Backtrolling

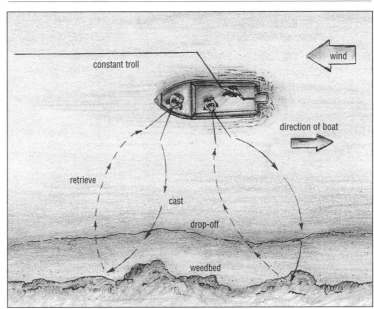

A combination approach usually used along the drop-off on a weed flat will work along any edge. You might also troll forward using a bowmount electric motor. The angler trolling should intermittently "pump" the spin rig forward, then let is slowly drift back, a prime triggering maneuver.

Presentation—A combination casting and trolling approach allows anglers to cover more water and trigger more active fish than either method individually. The boat driver trolls a 3/8-ounce Spin Rig and medium chub or shiner while watching the depthfinder to maintain contact with a drop-off on the edge of a weed flat. One or two additional anglers can cast 3/8- or 1/2-ounce Spin Rigs up onto the flat, retrieving the lures over and through weed clumps. When the lure loses contact with the weeds, pause to let the bait flutter down on a tight line. □

Weighted Bucktails For Muskies

RATHER THAN TOSSING THE SAME bucktails at the same speed as everyone else, consider something muskies haven't seen before. Most bucktails have bushy tails and large blade; a big cumbersome lure designed to entice a single large fish. But if you want to trigger lots of fish, consider lures at the opposite end of the spectrum. Small sparsely tied bucktails with small blades that can be reeled back to the boat at high speed because they are less water-resistant. This not only allows covering more water, but it adds a high-speed triggering effect that's deadly on muskies in heavily fished waters.

When—

Tackle— *Rod:* 7½-foot flippin' stick or muskie bucktail rod. *Reel:* wide-spool baitcasting reel. *Line:* 20-pound-test abrasion-resistant mono or 27-pound-test dacron.

Rigging—Start with a small- to medium-sized bucktail like a #5 Blue Fox Musky Buck, Windels Harasser, Fudally Musky Candy, Mepps Musky Killer, or Wahl's Little Eagle Tail. Thin the bucktail dressing by trimming hair at the collar, not the tips. Tips of hair provide all the action, and whole lengths of hair are more attractive and functional than hair stubs. Add 1/2 to 1 ounce of weight by removing the rubber core of a Rubbercor sinker and pinching the sinker around the main shaft or rear hook shank. Add a thin plastic worm tail to the forward hook to give the illusion of bulk without adding water-resistance.

Bucktail Options

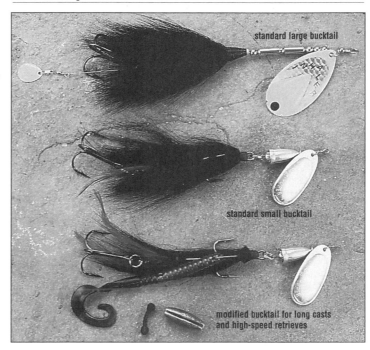

standard large bucktail

standard small bucktail

modified bucktail for long casts and high-speed retrieves

Presentation—Fish weighted bucktails in the same places you fish standard bucktails, but faster. Quickly cover points, bars, humps, reefs, and other muskie hangouts to catch active fish and locate neutral or negative muskies that may be triggered later in the day with a more subtle approach. Long casts and fast retrieves trigger fish that have already seen hundreds of lures. How fast? A bait can't be retrieved fast enough to pull it away from a fish that wants to eat it. Start the retrieve as soon as the lure hits the water, turning the reel handle as fast as possible. If the lure planes too high in the water column, creating a bulging wake on the surface, add more weight to the spinner shaft or use a smaller blade. □

Early Season Muskies

T HE FAMILIAR ADAGE FOR EARLY SEASON
remains, "find the warmest water possible and fish
small baits slowly." The truth is, however, this advice has
little bearing in reality. Most muskie openers in North
America—even on the Canadian Shield—coincide with
water temperatures in the 60°F range. Muskies are postspawn
and even into their early summer patterns. While the fish—
particularly larger females—aren't as aggressive as during
prime summer periods, they're aggressive enough to fall for
the same efficient fishing systems that often maximize fishing
successes during summer.

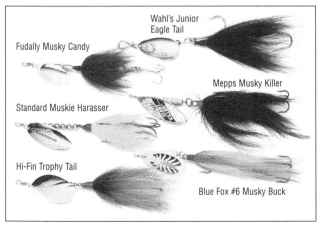

Wahl's Junior
Eagle Tail

Fudally Musky Candy

Mepps Musky Killer

Standard Muskie Harasser

Hi-Fin Trophy Tail

Blue Fox #6 Musky Buck

When—

Tackle— *Rod:* 6½- to 7½-foot
muskie bucktail rod. *Reel:* large-
capacity casting reel. *Line:* 27- to
36-pound-test dacron.

Rigging— Success during the early
season depends on your ability to fish
spots as quickly and efficiently as
possible with a lure that will trigger

the maximum number of fish. Many lures in your box will trigger fish, but few cover water as efficiently as a bucktail. Tie one on, cast it as far as you can, and retrieve it over as much good water as possible. If a small bait is easier to cast and retrieve all day—in other words if it keeps you fishing—then use it. Size just isn't the thing. Speed and efficiency and being in the right place are more important. Don't worry too much about color either. Choose a blade and bucktail combination that's highly visible— dark bucktails on dark days, lighter colors on bright days—and keep on fishing.

Early Season Transition To Summer Habitat

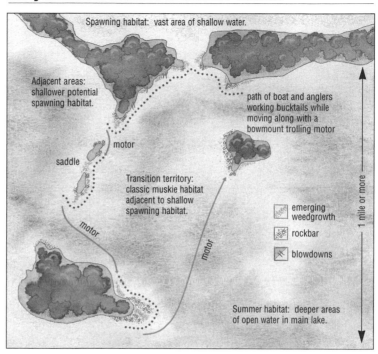

Spawning habitat: vast area of shallow water.

Adjacent areas: shallower potential spawning habitat.

path of boat and anglers working bucktails while moving along with a bowmount trolling motor

motor

saddle

Transition territory: classic muskie habitat adjacent to shallow spawning habitat.

motor

motor

emerging weedgrowth

rockbar

blowdowns

1 mile or more

Summer habitat: deeper areas of open water in main lake.

Location— Advice such as "fish the warmest water possible" suggests targeting bays and other backwater spots, when reality demands that muskies almost always are in transition territory on their way to summer holding areas by opening day. Recognition of where spawning territory lies, however, remains important in your search for transition spots as well as summer locations. Check your lake map for large shallow water areas, like bays and feeder creeks leading to backwaters. Deeper areas nearby attract muskies moving toward summer habitat—rocky reefs, island points and weed pockets, and weedbeds near the main lake. The best transition spots usually begin immediately adjacent to spawning habitat. □

Livebait For Muskies In Late Fall

Tail Spinner

L IVEBAIT WILL CATCH MUSKIES during difficult periods throughout the season, but it's particularly effective during fall. There's more to livebait fishing, however, than soaking a sucker beneath a float. The system described here is interactive—you see, feel, and react to what the fish are doing. Most importantly, though, it's productive—using livebait alone or in conjunction with casting will help maximize your catch in difficult conditions.

When—

Tackle— *Rod:* 6½- or 7-foot muskie bucktail rod. *Reel:* widespool baitcasting reel with a freespool clicker. *Line:* 30-pound-test abrasion-resistant mono.

Rigging— Connect a #6 snap to both ends of a small rubber band threaded through the nostrils of a 14- to 20-inch wild sucker. Wild white or redhorse suckers become frantic when a muskie is near, triggering fish that ignore a pond-raised baitfish. Slip a 4- to 6-inch 60-

pound-test stranded wire snell onto the snap. To the other end of the snell attach a 2/0 or 4/0 treble hook with a safety pin soldered to the shank. Slip the pin under the skin of the sucker. The snell should be slack so the bait can swim

Secure the hook along the side of the sucker with the safety pin.

Safety Pin Rig

Move into the wind to move baits to attract and trigger muskies. The best approach is to move the boat along slowly for about 5 feet, then let the sucker glide and swim. During the glide-swim, the sucker will tell you if a muskie's in the area. When a frantic bait isn't eaten, try speeding up the boat for 10 feet or so, followed by a glide-swim. If the fish still won't strike, try adding a tail spinner behind the anal fin of the sucker on the next pass. When one angler is casting and a muskie follows a lure back to the boat, get a livebait in the fish's face as quickly as possible. □

freely. On the hookset, the rubber band stretches and the exposed hook pulls free of the bait and into the muskie's mouth.

Presentation— In prime spots, take at least three passes thorough an area, running tight to the drop-off edge on one pass, about 60 feet out on another pass, and about 120 feet out from the edge on the final pass. Each new pass usually requires that baits be picked up as the boat quickly motors to the original downwind position to begin the pass. Each pass may also require a new combination of rigging options. Passes out from the edge made directly into the wind may also call for a downline and planer board lines on each side of the boat.

Bait Tactics

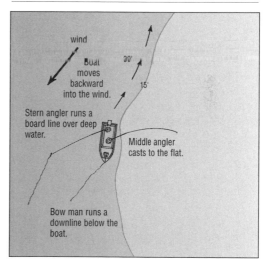

wind

Boat moves backward into the wind.

Stern angler runs a board line over deep water.

Middle angler casts to the flat.

Bow man runs a downline below the boat.

Jerkbaits For River Muskies

MUSKIES ARE MUSKIES, wherever they swim. Fish in rivers eat bucktails, plugs, and topwaters just as their still-water cousins do. They follow baits back to the boat, too; sometimes striking a well-executed figure eight, but more often swimming away. Because river muskies behave

Provoker

Reef Hog

enough like lake muskies, most anglers fish for them exactly the same way. But paying attention to small presentation details can mean the difference between triggering strikes and attracting follows. Fishing for muskies in rivers is a simple but exact science.

When—

Gliding jerkbaits excel for muskies in rivers.

Tackle— *Rod:* 6- to 7-foot muskie jerkbait rod. *Reel:* large-capacity baitcasting reel. *Line:* 27- or 36-pound-test dacron.

Location— To find muskies in rivers, look for deeper water—pools or holes. Muskies usually relate to cover or bottom structure in or adjacent to pools. Cover and bottom structure divert current. Muskies lie in the slack water behind obstructions. Heavy current and high water levels often push them tight to the bank behind cover breaks such as fallen timber or large rocks, or behind structural elements like points. Low water moves them away from the bank into the middle of pools. In normal water levels, muskies move where they wish. Prime lies, however, remain in slack water behind cover or bottom structure. Secondary lies may be found at the head or tailout of pools or on flats adjacent to pools.

Presentation— Most anglers float downriver, rifling casts into spots before they get to them. Wait. Drift even with a spot, have a look at it as you drift by, then make a 45° cast back upstream to the head of the spot. Good boat control is critical. Work the bait back to the boat with the current. Don't let it swing, even on a slow retrieve. Once your bait starts moving upstream at the end of a drift, your chance for a strike is diminished.

After casting, face the bait and hold your rod tip directly in front of you at a 30° to 45° angle down toward the water. With a tight line pull, not snap, the rod tip toward the water about a foot. As the bait glides, immediately reel in the slack line and move your rod tip back to the starting position. During summer, your retrieve sequence might go snap, snap, snap at 3- to 5-second intervals. During fall, the sequence should be pull-glide, pull-glide, at 5- to 7-second intervals. □

Casting Angle

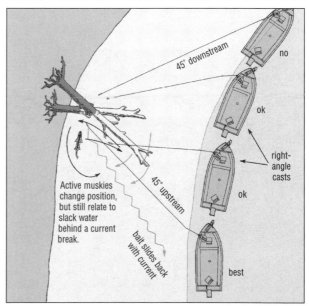

Active muskies change position, but still relate to slack water behind a current break.

45° downstream — no

ok

right-angle casts

45° upstream — ok

bait slides back with current — best

MUSKIE

Trolling Jerkbaits For Muskies

TRACKING STUDIES INDICATE THAT MUSKIES SUSPEND more than most anglers think. They also move long distances across open water toward prime feeding locations. They may regularly move miles per day, spending short periods on shallow water structures, and then back across open water toward their next destination. If you're casting to shallow structure and not seeing fish, or fish are following your lure without striking, it may be time to give trolling a try.

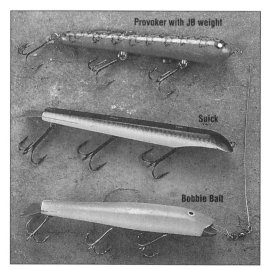

Provoker with JB weight

Suick

Bobbie Bait

When—

Tackle— *Rod:* 6- to 7-foot heavy-action muskie jerkbait rod. *Reel:* large-capacity baitcasting reel. *Line:* 36-pound-test dacron.

Location— During late summer and fall, muskies frequently roam between structural elements. Troll jerkbaits along a weededge; along or over rock bars or sand bars; along timber edges; over flats filled with fallen timber; and over sunken humps. In rivers, lakes, and reservoirs—almost anywhere muskies swim—trolled jerkbaits are an option.

Presentation—

For trolling, jerkbaits fall into two categories: those with a gliding side-to-side action and those with a diving up-and-down action. Gliding jerkbaits don't move consistently unless you stand up while trolling. To keep them working steadily from side-to-side, point your rod tip down

Late Summer And Fall Locations

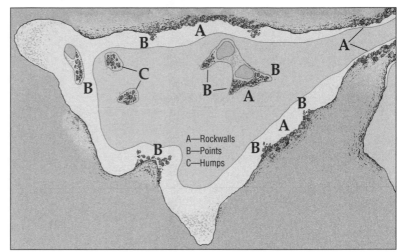

Many potential muskie locations in late summer and fall are associated with the main-lake basin. Trolling multiple structural elements dramatically increases your odds of contacting muskies.

and jerk the rod tip down about 6 inches. This sends the plug darting several feet left or right. Occasionally, it'll dive down or come to the surface. If you try to do this while sitting down, the bait will dart too erratically for even the most aggressive fish to hit.

With a diving jerkbait, sit down and hold the rod tip up or to the side. Don't troll too fast, but do keep your speed steady. Trolled slowly, a bait alternately dives a bit and floats up a bit, as the rod tip is jerked forward or up about a foot.

Let the rod tip slowly drift back to its original position after each jerk. The forward movement of the boat keeps the line tight. A faster trolling speed makes the bait dive to a certain depth, but diminishes its up and down movement. The result is a jerk-forward, stop, jerk-forward, stop action. Increase lure depth by letting out more line, switching to lighter line, or using wire line. Also experiment with weighted jerkbaits, or weight standard baits by drilling holes and adding lead. □

Locating Trophy Chain Pickerel

THE CHAIN PICKEREL IS THE LARGEST PICKEREL species, which is, in turn, the smallest member of the Esocidae family of fishes. Biologists lump them together with pike and muskies, but few anglers consider them worthy of the same attention. They average only a pound or two in most waters and usually are caught on presentations intended for bass and pike. But what pickerel lack in size they make up for with their aggressive attitude. These scrappy sportfish hit fast-moving spoons after an early summer cold front as readily as they inhale shiners suspended below tip-ups in the middle of winter. Big fish are always a challenge, but pickerel of any size are fun.

Chain Pickerel Range

When—

Tackle— *Rod:* 6- to 7-foot medium-power spinning rod. *Reel:* medium-capacity spinning reel. *Line:* 4- to 8-pound-test abrasion-resistant mono.

Rigging— Despite the pickerel's sharp teeth, wire leaders are seldom necessary. Check your line frequently and retie when it shows signs of abrasion. Large pickerel feed almost entirely on fish, so live minnows and minnow-imitating lures are effective baits. A #1 light-wire hook weighted with lead shot and baited with a 3- to 5-inch shiner or chub is effective down to about 10 feet. For deeper water, add a #10 barrel swivel and a 1/4-ounce slip sinker above a 12- to 24-inch mono leader. A weedless spoon dressed with a piece of pork or plastic is the most popular artificial, though soft-plastic stickbaits, spinnerbaits, and minnowbaits also are effective.

Location—Chain pickerel inhabit small natural lakes, creeks, and quiet river backwaters along the Atlantic Coast from Maine to Florida and west to Louisiana and Arkansas. Like northern pike, pickerel are ambush predators, often lying motionless for hours until a small perch or other preyfish ventures too close. From fall through spring, pickerel often relate to emergent and submergent weeds from shore out to about 10 feet. During summer, however, big fish move to deep weededges on breaks that gradually taper from 10 to about 20 feet of water. Big pickerel, like big pike, seem to prefer cooler water than what smaller fish prefer, and they often hold just above or in the thermocline.

Presentation—Cast livebait rigs into pockets and cuts in the weededge and let the bait sink to the bottom. Work the bait slowly back to the boat, dragging the sinker across the bottom as you would for smallmouth. When a pickerel

Pickerel Location

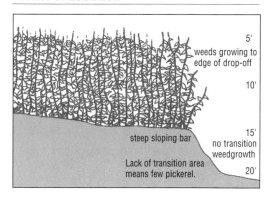

weeds growing to edge of drop-off 5'

10'

steep sloping bar

15'
no transition weedgrowth

Lack of transition area means few pickerel.

20'

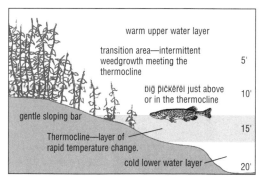

warm upper water layer

transition area—intermittent weedgrowth meeting the thermocline 5'

big pickerel just above or in the thermocline 10'

gentle sloping bar

Thermocline—layer of rapid temperature change. 15'

cold lower water layer 20'

grabs the bait, however, don't let him run. Set the hook immediately and pull him away from the weeds. Retrieve spoons and other lures parallel to the weededge. Pickerel in shallow water attack baits presented from the surface down to the bottom. In deeper water, however, they seldom strike surface baits. □

Blue Catfish From Cold Water

VETERAN CATMEN KNOW THAT BLUE cats, more than channels or flatheads, are creatures of big rivers and impoundments. They know, too, that big blues like more current than either of their whiskered cousins. Until recently, however, few people were aware of the blue cat's love of cold water. Instead of sticking their belly to the bottom of a hole for the winter, these fish continue to forage in chutes of swift current when water temperatures drop to 35°F. In river-run reservoirs across much of the blue cat's range, the period from December through March may be the best time to tangle with a monster blue.

When—

Tackle— *Rod:* 6- to 8-foot medium-heavy-power casting rod. *Reel:* large-capacity casting reel with a freespool clicker. *Line:* 20- to 40-pound-test abrasion-resistant mono.

Rigging— A basic slip rig consisting of a 1- to 6-ounce egg sinker sliding on the main line, which is tied to a 1- to 3-foot leader consisting of a hook, line, and swivel. Several 1-inch cubes of cutbait pack neatly on a 7/0 Kahle-style hook and don't roll as much in current as a long strip of bait.

Location—During winter and early spring, big blue cats run the river channel, feeding along channel ledges. They rarely move onto adjacent shallow flats. Even hot-water discharges don't attract big blue cats, although they do draw one of the blue cat's favorite baitfish, the skipjack herring. A discharge area is a prime spot to gather fresh herring for cutbait.

Area A—The head of a narrow river section before the river widens and flattens is a prime area for blue cats that hesitate to move farther upriver into decreasing current. Use sonar to run upriver along the channel ledge, looking for nooks and debris that attract and hold fish. A particularly good area is where the ledge begins to push away from the bank to form a large shallow flat.

Area B—The entire ledge is a potential holding area for blue cats. Try the ledge area near the final barge tie-off. Should be a big eddy here, too. Note also how the ledge pushes away from the bank near the beginning of the discharge area—good spot. The head of a deep channel area as it pushes into a shallower area is another hot spot for big blues.

Area C—First check the ledge area where the shallow flat extends into the channel below the discharge inlet. Then note how the flat cuts back toward the bluff bank, creating another possible holding area. Be sure to run along the ledge near the bluff bank—limestone outcroppings are particularly craggy and difficult to fish, but often hold big blues. □

Typical Flowing Reservoir

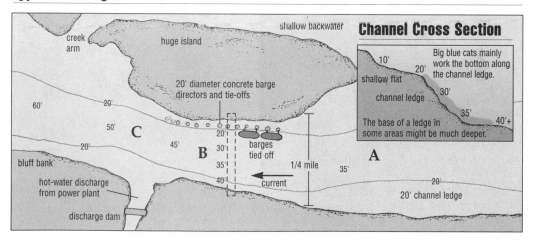

Simple Strategies For Big Flatheads

A T THE BEGINNING OF SUMMER, ONCE THE WATER settles in a river and flatheads settle into the biggest, deepest, most cover-laden holes, lots of carp will be working along cut banks at night. A month later, if the water stays down, the hole will be silent. The carp are gone. Eaten, along with bullheads and most other sizable prey in the hole. Won't catch many channel cats under 5 pounds in there either. Dead and gone except for a few smiling flatheads. They're probably big and definitely hungry. Get a large, lively bait in there at night to catch them.

Flatheads In Reservoirs

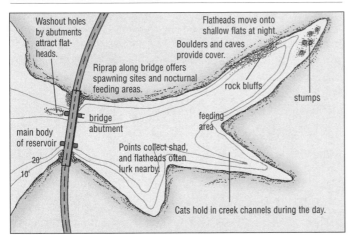

Washout holes by abutments attract flat-heads.

Flatheads move onto shallow flats at night.

Boulders and caves provide cover.

Riprap along bridge offers spawning sites and nocturnal feeding areas.

rock bluffs

stumps

bridge abutment

feeding area

main body of reservoir

20'

10'

Points collect shad, and flatheads often lurk nearby.

Cats hold in creek channels during the day.

When—

Tackle— *Rod:* 6- to 7½-foot heavy-power casting rod. *Reel:* wide-spool baitcasting reel with a freespool clicker. *Line:* 20- to 50-pound-test abrasion-resistant mono.

Rigging—Set rigs for flatheads consist of a strong 3/0 to 9/0 hook, a 1- to 6-ounce bell sinker, and a bead between them to cushion the knot. Sharpen the hook and slip it though flesh just below and behind the dorsal fin of a big, lively baitfish. Suckers raised in bait ponds don't last as long and don't attract as many fish as wild 10- to 15-inch suckers. Green sunfish, drum, bullheads, and carp also are fine bait.

Presentation—On small- and medium-size rivers, look for deep outside bends that may drop to 18 or 20 feet, or midriver holes of 10 to 12 feet. Even on big rivers, flatheads don't seem to hold deeper than about 30 feet in summer. On any spot, the more cover the better. After dark, flatheads sometimes move shallow to forage, seeking suckers and shad that seek protection in skinny water.

Finding flatheads in reservoirs may seem more difficult, but they still follow a predictable routine. In early summer, flatheads follow baitfish into creek arms. Set baits on flats along the creek channel and across the flat. If the channel is too far to cast to, fish from a boat or use a boat to place your baits and then return to shore. Later in summer, move to flats at the head of the creek arm where it meets the main reservoir. □

Flatheads In Rivers

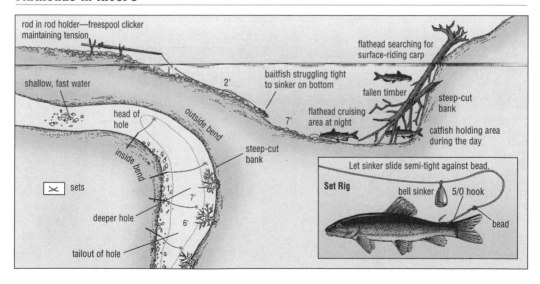

Float Rigs For Catfish

USING FLOATS IS ONE OF THE simplest but most potent ways to catch more and bigger catfish. Two mistaken ideas keep most catfishermen from ever considering them. First, many people think catfish feed exclusively on the bottom. Second, many believe floats are good only for suspending baits above bottom. But floats can be used to improve presentation, deliver and hold a bait in a particular area, and indicate bites. Primarily, however, a float helps drift a bait accurately and keep it moving smoothly along the bottom.

When—

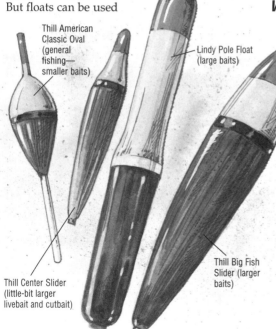

Thill American Classic Oval (general fishing—smaller baits)

Lindy Pole Float (large baits)

Thill Center Slider (little-bit larger livebait and cutbait)

Thill Big Fish Slider (larger baits)

Tackle— *Rod:* 7- to 12-foot medium- to heavy-power casting or spinning rod with a moderately fast action. *Reel:* wide-spool reel. *Line:* 12- to 30-pound-test mono.

Rigging— Tie a five-turn uni-knot around your main line, using the same or slightly heavier line. This serves as an adjustable float stop. Slip on a small bead, followed by the slip float, hook, and lead shot. Now slide the stop knot and slip float up your line so the float suspends the bait near bottom.

To anchor a big livebait for flatheads, tie on a swivel about 20 inches above a 3/0 to 7/0 hook. Add a 1- to 4-ounce egg sinker (depending on the size of the livebait) above the swivel. A big float is needed to hold up this rig.

Presentation—Float rigs are particularly deadly in rivers when they're drifted through the tail end of a riffle and into the beginning of a hole, along and around snags, and over flats such as the run at the tailout of holes. In all of these situations, livebait works well during early and late season, cutbait all season, and stinkbaits during summer. In deep slack areas in rivers and in reservoirs, ponds, and lakes, use floats to suspend cutbait for channel and blue cats running shad, or to suspend big livebaits for flathead cats.

Large livebaits suspended beneath big floats are deadly for flatheads in rivers and reservoirs. No need to get the bait extra deep. Indeed, just about 5 feet down often does it, even when the water's over 10 feet deep. Flatheads spend a lot of time attacking fish riding near the surface. They can feel vibrations from the struggling bait. □

Float Rigging For Flatheads

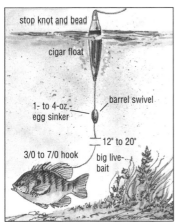

stop knot and bead

cigar float

1- to 4-oz. egg sinker

barrel swivel

3/0 to 7/0 hook

12" to 20"

big live- bait

Slip Float Rigging

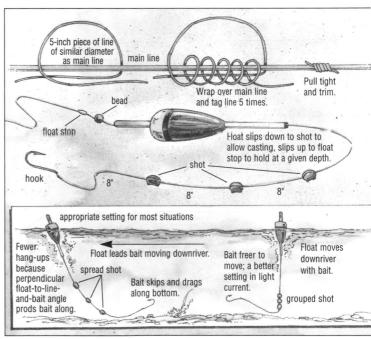

5-inch piece of line of similar diameter as main line

main line

Wrap over main line and tag line 5 times.

Pull tight and trim.

bead

float stop

Float slips down to shot to allow casting, slips up to float stop to hold at a given depth.

shot

hook

8"

8"

8"

appropriate setting for most situations

Fewer hang-ups because perpendicular float-to-line-and-bait angle prods bait along.

Float leads bait moving downriver

spread shot

Bait skips and drags along bottom.

Bait freer to move; a better setting in light current.

Float moves downriver with bait.

grouped shot

Catfish Location In Small Rivers

T HE EASIEST WAY TO UNDERSTAND CATFISH location in rivers is to look at small streams. Small streams are easier to get to know because the catfish's world is compressed into a small area. In a large river, major holes may be half a mile apart. On a small stream, however, half a mile might contain 10 holes. You can move and see lots of water. More importantly, the continuing combination of riffles, holes, and runs, and the cover elements that may exist in them are obvious. Small rivers offer the quickest education in river anatomy and how catfish relate to it.

Riffle-Hole-Run

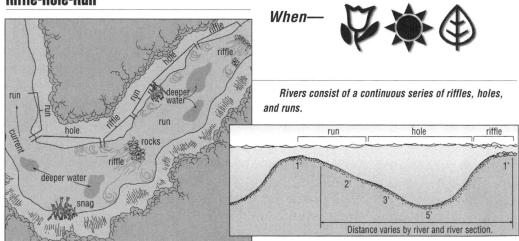

When—

Rivers consist of a continuous series of riffles, holes, and runs.

Distance varies by river and river section.

Tackle— *Rod:* 7- to 12-foot casting or spinning rod. *Reel:* medium-capacity baitcasting or spinning reel. *Line:* 10- to 20-pound-test abrasion-resistant mono.

Location— Riffles form when a river washes over a hard bottom. A pool of water builds at the head of a riffle, eventually overflowing and pushing over the constricted area like water forced through the nozzle of a hose. The force of current flowing against the softer substrate at the end of a riffle scours a hole. Holes are the home of catfish. The depth of a hole varies according to current velocity and the size of the river, but all holes are deeper and wider than riffle and run areas in the same section of stream. Holes gradually become shallower at their downstream end as current slows and suspended materials settle to the river bottom. The tail end of a hole becomes a run—a river flat.

Catfish often move upstream to smaller water during spring and early summer, then back downstream into bigger water during late summer and early fall. During winter, catfish must gather in holes with sufficient depth, current, and oxygen to sustain them throughout the cold-water period. Such holes are most likely in downriver sections. Flatheads rarely move more than one tributary away from a major river, while channel cats may move into tiny creeks several tributaries removed from a major river. Blue cats, even more than flatheads, are fish of big rivers. Smaller blues may push upriver into the beginning stretches of tributary streams, but the biggest blues usually stay in big water. □

Holding Areas In A Typical Hole

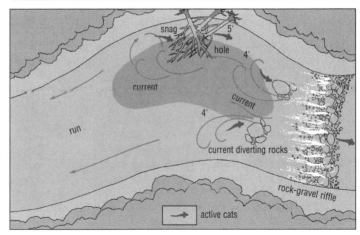

Inactive cats usually hold in the snag or in deeper water in a hole. Active cats feed near the snag but just as likely leave the snag and (1) move ahead of the riffle to feed in the fast slick water; (2) find a spot to hold and wait for food below the riffle; or (3) roam the hole searching for food.

Sour Bait For Channel Cats

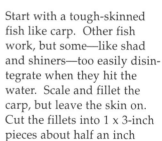

SOUR BAIT, PUT MILDLY, IS FISH FLESH turned rotten, rancid, and ripe. When fish die in the winter, they don't immediately decompose in the cold water. When temperatures rise in the spring, gases inside these fish expand and they float to the surface. These floaters are driven by wind and current to predictable places—coves on the windward side of lakes, cuts in reservoir creek arms, and eddies in rivers. Catfish concentrate in these areas, gorging on these springtime delicacies.

When—

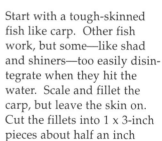

Tackle— *Rod:* 7- to 12-foot casting or spinning rod. *Reel:* medium-capacity spinning or baitcasting reel. *Line:* 14- to 20-pound-test mono.

Rigging— Natural sour bait is abundant in early spring, but making your own is easy.

Start with a tough-skinned fish like carp. Other fish work, but some—like shad and shiners—too easily disintegrate when they hit the water. Scale and fillet the carp, but leave the skin on. Cut the fillets into 1 x 3-inch pieces about half an inch thick. Pack the pieces into a glass jar, leaving an inch open at the top. Add a few teaspoons of water to accelerate fermentation. Screw on the lid loosely—too tight and expanding gases may cause the jar to explode. Bury the jar in 6 inches of soil that receives several hours of sunlight per day. Let the bait fester a week or two and it's ready. Run the hook once through a piece of sour bait, leaving the hook point exposed.

Presentation— Fish the bait in areas where natural sours tend to collect. It's equally effective drifted below a float or anchored on a slip rig. During spring, the best catfishing often is from midday and on. Several warm spring days along with a stable river level signals good fishing. As spring moves

toward summer, fresh cutbait begins to outfish sours, although sours will continue to produce cats—especially smaller cats—all season. □

Location In Small Rivers

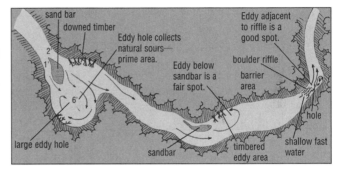

sand bar
downed timber
Eddy hole collects natural sours— prime area.
Eddy below sandbar is a fair spot.
Eddy adjacent to riffle is a good spot.
boulder riffle
barrier area
hole
large eddy hole
sandbar
timbered eddy area
shallow fast water

Location In Reservoirs

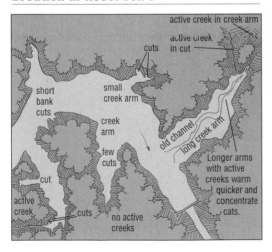

active creek in creek arm
active creek in cut
cuts
short bank cuts
small creek arm
creek arm
old channel
long creek arm
few cuts
cut
active creek
cuts
no active creeks
Longer arms with active creeks warm quicker and concentrate cats.

Location In Lakes

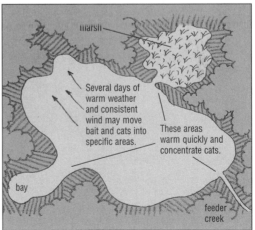

marsh
Several days of warm weather and consistent wind may move bait and cats into specific areas.
These areas warm quickly and concentrate cats.
bay
feeder creek

Bullheads During Spring

Bullheads are the first fish caught by many anglers. Prized by children, but often forgotten or at least overlooked by fishermen who pursue more "serious" species. Bullheads will never be the stuff of bass tournaments, expensive advertising campaigns, and high-tech gadgets. Bullheads are just plain bullheads and that's good enough. Whether on the line or in the pan, they possess a magic we never outgrow.

The Best Jigheads

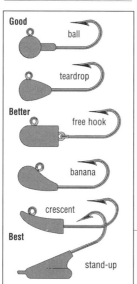

Good
ball

teardrop

Better
free hook

banana

crescent

Best
stand-up

When—

Leadhead jigs filled with worms and fished stationary on the bottom are great for bullheads.

Tackle— *Rod:* 6- to 7½-foot medium-power spinning rod. *Reel:* medium-capacity spinning reel. *Line:* 8- to 12-pound-test mono.

Rigging— The same set and float rigs used for catfish catch bullheads, but leadhead jigs may be the best option of all. Choose a jig with a 1/0 or 2/0 hook, and add a night crawler or two. Thread worms onto the hook loosely, leaving the hook point exposed and the head of the crawler free to wriggle. Bullheads eat down to the leadhead and then have a difficult time swallowing it. By then you have 'em. The head of the jig also makes a good handle for unhooking fish. Stand-up jigs with wedge heads work best.

Location— In spring, bullheads are drawn to warmer water and more abundant food in backwater areas. In the lake illustrated here, bullheads from the main body of water move through the connecting canal into the backwater. Once in the backwater, some of them move into the slough—primarily black bullhead territory. Yellow and and brown bullheads usually remain in the backwater.
A reverse migration occurs after the spawn. Some black bullheads, though, may remain in the backwater throughout the summer if current prevents excessive water stagnation.

Bullheads often concentrate in funnel areas like *Canals A* and *B*. Bullheads must move thorough these areas, and current tends to concentrate washed in food to attract and hold them. Vegetation breaks like the bulrushes along the north and south shorelines of the backwater also gather fish. Bullheads travel the front face of these spots, but tend to concentrate where vegetation stops (*C*, *D*, *E*, and *F*) and where it forms points. Areas immediately outside *Canal A* attract bullheads after they spawn. Fish the front face of reeds and cabbage, plus the coontail flats and the outside edge of the deeper weeds. □

Backwater Bullheads

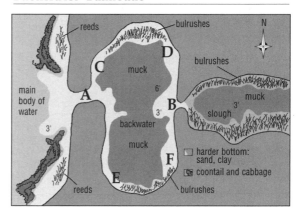

Concentration Spots

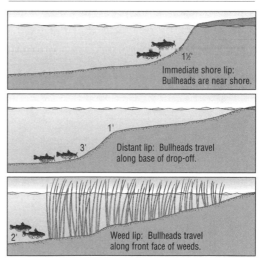

Immediate shore lip: Bullheads are near shore.

Distant lip: Bullheads travel along base of drop-off.

Weed lip: Bullheads travel along front face of weeds.

Bait Rigs For Carp

THE MERITS OF CARP ARE EASY TO extol: Superior intelligence. Large carp are simply the wariest of all freshwater fish, by reason not just of superior brain power in combination with sheer age, but through their acute senses of hearing, feeling, taste, and vision. Immense size. Fish over 100 pounds probably exist, and 30s, 40s, and 50s are common in some waters. Immense power. A 20-pounder will routinely crack off 50 yards of 10-pound line, and will do it again and again. Supreme beauty. Specimens from clear water are stunning. Such views are difficult for many North American anglers to accept because they've heard otherwise for so long. But for the enlightened who target this supreme gamefish, no other fish seems quite so worthy of pursuit.

When—

Tackle— *Rod:* 7- to 12-foot medium-heavy-power spinning rod. *Reel:* medium-capacity spinning reel. *Line:* 8- to 12-pound-test mono.

Hair Rigs

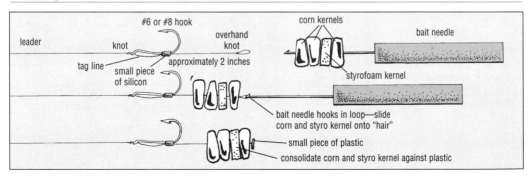

Rigging—Set rigs for carp are similar to those used for catfish and other species. The simplest rigging involves a sliding bell sinker stopped by a bead against a small swivel. The leader can be an 18- to 24-inch segment of either mono or fused-filament line. The business end of the leader is a hair rig that rests on the bottom or slightly above with the aid of a small piece of styrofoam. For bait, it's tough to beat hard field corn. Cover it with water and allow it to soak for a few days, then boil it for an hour just before you fish. A teaspoon of vanilla or other flavoring for each pint of bait often attracts more carp.

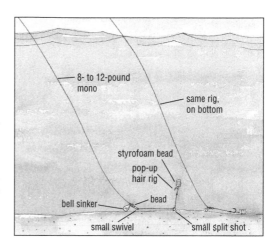

Presentation—Where legal, baiting or chumming greatly improves your odds of catching numbers of carp. If the bait is grouped in one spot, however, fish will quickly consume it and move on. Spread the bait out in an area roughly the size of a tennis court and it will attract carp to the area and keep them occupied for a longer time. A small slingshot can be used to launch baits further from shore, but still within casting distance of a long rod. It doesn't matter where you place your rig within the spread, but often hot spots will become apparent as the day progresses. Cast to different spots after you hook or miss a fish to locate the best areas. □

Baiting An Area In Lakes

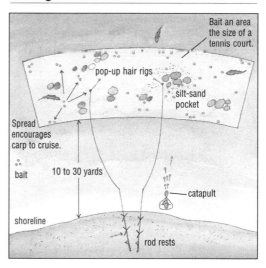

Carp On The Flats

ARP ARE THE BONEFISH OF FRESH-water. Both are wary, suspicious, and quick to spook at the slightest provocation. Both cruise shallow flats in search of food. Bonefish are harder to see, but no harder to hook. Both are prone to strike lures and flies that imitate crustaceans, insects, and small fish. Carp are bigger and more powerful. Bones are faster. But the primary difference is that bonefish are prized—even adored—while carp are maligned. Ignored by all but a few anglers who have discovered the thrill of sight-fishing for carp in clear water. It's a demanding, challenging pursuit that requires patience, casting skill, and attention to detail.

When—

Tackle—

Rod: 6½- to 7½-foot medium- to medium-heavy-power spinning rod. *Reel:* medium-capacity spinning reel with a smooth drag. *Line:* 6- or 8-pound-test abrasion-resistant mono.

Marabou, bucktail, or plastic trailers mimic what carp feed on and slow the drop rate of a jig. Simple nymph and streamer patterns and smaller marabou jigs on the end of a fly line drop even slower.

Rigging—Choosing an appropriate jig requires trial and error and close observation. Active carp take jigs on the drop—the longer a jig hangs in the strike zone the better your chance for a strike. The perfect jig for hang time is light (1/32 to 1/16 ounce) with hair, feathers, or plastic aiding the parachute effect. A light jig might drop too slowly, however, when carp are really on the move; and a light jig becomes impossible to cast or control in wind. Under those conditions, go to a 1/8- or a 1/4-ounce jig.

Location—Carp in clear lakes and reservoirs spread out during summer, using main-lake flats in the 2- to 10-foot range extending from islands and shore-lines. Bottom composition doesn't seem to matter. If it's a big shallow area, carp probably live there. But hard-bottom flats and rocky bays where carp can't muddy the water make it easier for anglers to spot cruising fish and for carp to locate jigs.

Carping The Flats

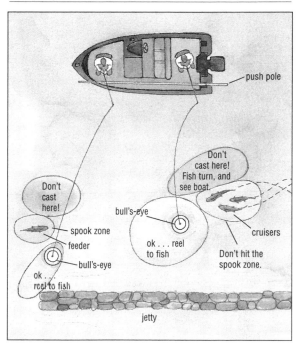

Presentation—The primary casting target is an area 4 to 10 feet ahead and slightly beyond the path of the fish. Carp have good peripheral vision. They will often turn 90 degrees to take a jig, and a short cast could cause them to turn and see the boat. A jig presented too close will also spook them. If the cast drops too far in front of a carp, pop the jig 2 or 3 feet off bottom and let it fall again as the fish passes. If this fails to trigger a strike, try slowly swimming the jig right along the bottom or several feet up. What carp are focused on might be difficult to determine, but often a pattern develops. Experimenting with different retrieves and various weights and styles of jig can be critical when carp are feeding selectively. □

Understanding Buffalo

THE THREE BUFFALO SPECIES—
bigmouth, smallmouth, and black—are among the largest fish available to freshwater anglers, with all species commonly exceeding 40 pounds in some areas. Their potential size attracts European visitors eager to test tackle on fish that superficially look like carp and can sometimes be taken with similar techniques. But these tremendous sportfish are ignored by most native anglers.

When—

Tackle— *Rod:* 7- to 12-foot medium-heavy-power spinning rod. *Reel:* large-capacity spinning reel. *Line:* 14- to 20-pound-test abrasion-resistant mono.

Species— The bigmouth buffalo is the largest and most widespread of the three species. They are the only sucker with a terminal mouth instead of the typical subterminal position like suckers and carp. This feature and many long gill rakers enable the bigmouth to filter zooplankton from the water. Large schools often swim through midwater areas to feed.

Smallmouth buffalo are widespread in the central United States. Their body is deeper and

Bigmouth Buffalo

Smallmouth Buffalo

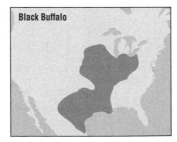

Black Buffalo

more slab-sided than the rounder bigmouth. Smallmouths typically inhabit clearer, faster waters than bigmouths, though they may school together. They're opportunistic bottom feeders, taking larval insects, clams, invertebrates, and vegetation. They often inhale a mouthful of gravel, separate edible items, then spit out the rock.

Black buffalo appear intermediate between the other two species in habitat preference and appearance, which led commercial fishermen to label it the mongrel buffalo. Its limited range and abundance, and its confusion with other species, limits our knowledge of the black buffalo's habitat preferences. It seems, however, to prefer deeper water and stronger currents than do the other two species.

Rigging— When anglers fishing for walleyes, panfish, or carp catch a large buffalo, the battle is exhilarating if not exhausting. Bigmouth buffalo often take jigs tipped with minnows fished in channels or near wing dams and other current breaks. For best results especially for smallmouth and black buffalo, keep baits on the bottom. Drift rigs consisting of a dropper line with lead shot and a leader with a small hook baited with a worm or paste bait work well for checking spots in steams and midsize rivers. In large rivers, anchor baits with a bell sinker on a three-way swivel rig. Natural food items like insect larvae, native snails, and earthworms are the best baits.

Presentation— Shore fishing works best when buffalo congregate in backwaters. Set rods in holders with sensitive bite indicators. Like carp, buffalo bite delicately but make long, powerful runs once hooked, so the drag must be smooth and correctly set. While anglers occasionally land big buffalo on light tackle, plan to gear up in waters with 30-, 40-, or even 50-pound fish. □

Buffalo Rigs

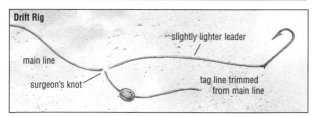

Drift Rig

slightly lighter leader

main line

surgeon's knot

tag line trimmed from main line

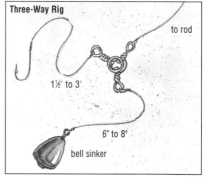

Three-Way Rig

to rod

1½' to 3'

6" to 8"

bell sinker

Catching And Preparing Spring Suckers

Suckers, IN THEIR MANY VARIETIES, are everything an "alternative" fish should be. A bullet shaped and muscular feisty redhorse, pushing three pounds, will quickly peel off 15 feet of drag if you're running 6-pound line—enough to make you wonder if your rig will hold. Then it burrows and shakes, runs another time or two, and perhaps jumps. Redhorse are beauties to behold, too—perfectly scaled packages of sunset gold and vibrant red, with dark, deep eyes. Fish from clean, cold, clear water are wonderful table fare. They're often smoked and pickled, but they also make the finest fish patties you'll ever taste.

When—

Tackle— *Rod:* 6- to 7-foot light-power spinning rod. *Reel:* small spinning reel. *Line:* 6-pound-test mono.

Rigging— Rigs for not-so-savvy suckers can be as simple as a #6 or #8 hook to hold a portion of night crawler, and a lead shot pinched eight inches up the line to keep the bait near the bottom. A dropper rig constructed with a surgeon's knot works best for finicky fish. Using a 2-foot section of line, tie a triple surgeon's knot so the short tag ends are about 6 inches long. Trim off one of the short tags and pinch a lead shot on the end of the other, which now serves as a dropper. Add a hook to the long tag end and bait with the tail section of a crawler.

Location— Most rivers and streams progress in a continuous series of riffle-hole-run structure, the riffle being a shallow area where the water runs quickly over rock rubble, then slides into a deeper hole, usually with a sand bottom. At the tailout of the hole, sand settles and the hole becomes a river flat that runs until it hits hard bottom and forms another riffle. Suckers usually hold along the edge of holes and in eddies, which are areas where an obstruction causes current to reverse itself. If the water is running slowly through the core of the hole, suckers will be there. □

Lucia's Favorite Fish Cakes

Recipe— Mix one part mashed russet potatoes with three parts ground sucker. For a hungry group of four, use about three pounds of sucker and a pound of spuds. Add a tablespoon of lemon juice, a pinch of salt and pepper, a tablespoon of Worcestershire sauce, and 3 tablespoons of minced scallion. If the mixture seems too thick, add a little milk. Shape mixture into round cakes about 1/2 inch thick. Lightly dust with flour and sauté in butter over medium heat approximately 3 minutes per side.

Fishing For Creek Chubs

Bait Rig

Flies

Jigs

A CROSS THE EASTERN HALF OF THE UNITED States, young anglers pursue creek chubs with the same vigor mature anglers reserve for stream trout. And why not? Chubs are widely distributed, aggressive throughout most of the year, and are fun to catch on light tackle. Best of all, a 10-year-old with a cane pole and a can of worms can catch as many chubs as a fly-fisherman armed with a bamboo rod and boxful of flies. While chubs seldom are harvested for food, their hardiness and relatively large size make them a favorite bait for catfish, bass, and pike.

When—

Tackle— *Rod:* 5- to 6-foot ultralight spinning rod. *Reel:* small-capacity spinning reel. *Line:* 4-pound-test mono.

Rigging— Creek chubs are efficient omnivores, eating everything from plankton to insects to smaller minnows. The most popular rig for large chubs consists of a lead shot pinched on the line 6 inches or so above a #10 to #6 light-wire hook. Tip the hook with a small piece of night crawler, a live nymph, or a maggot or two. Small artificial lures also catch chubs, especially

1/32- to 1/64-ounce jigs dressed with a tuft of marabou. Chubs also are terrific fun on a fly rod, routinely striking nymphs, dry flies, and small streamers intended for trout.

Location— Chubs often are found in small- to medium-size rivers and lakes with shallow rocky shorelines, but they prefer the small, clear, hard-bottomed streams that crisscross the eastern half of North America. Like trout, creek chubs are built for the rigors of current and often seek out the same kind of holding and feeding areas. Riffles, deep pools, and eddies formed by current breaks are top locations. In streams with long shallow runs, every good sized pool may hold hundreds of chubs.

Presentation— When chubs are actively feeding— as they are throughout much of the summer— you'll quickly fill a bait bucket by drifting natural or artificial baits through the tail end of riffles into the head of a hole. Cast baits across and slightly

upstream, and hold your rod tip high for the longest drift and to detect subtle bites. When the fish are holding in deep water and seem reluctant to pursue moving baits, add another shot or two to a livebait rig and cast into the core of the hole. □

Creek Chub Distribution

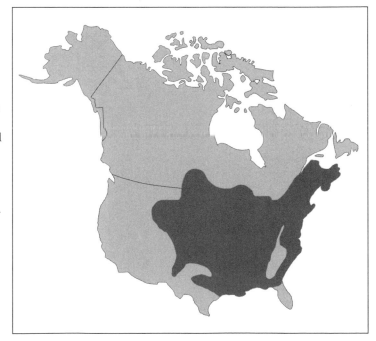

Trolling Livebait For Striped Bass

A FTER SPAWNING AT WATER temperatures from the high 50s to mid-60's, striped bass often run along steep banks where shad are spawning. This short activity period can bring explosive fishing with topwaters, crankbaits, or bucktails and spoons burned just below the surface. When adult shad move offshore after spawning, however, stripers follow. As surface temperatures approach 75°F, large stripers drop into deeper water. Trolling is the most efficient way to get a bait in front of these suspended fish in big water.

Bait Rigs

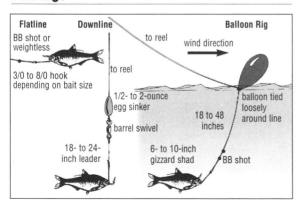

Flatline
BB shot or weightless
3/0 to 8/0 hook depending on bait size
18- to 24-inch leader

Downline
to reel
1/2- to 2-ounce egg sinker
barrel swivel

Balloon Rig
to reel
wind direction
balloon tied loosely around line
18 to 48 inches
6- to 10-inch gizzard shad
BB shot

When—

Tackle— *Rod:* 7- to 7½-foot heavy-power casting rod. *Reel:* large-capacity baitcasting reel. *Line:* 17- to 30-pound-test abrasion-resistant mono.

Downlines— Downlines consist of a sinker weighing 3/4 ounce set on the line above a barrel swivel, a leader from 4 to 6 feet long, and a single 3/0 hook. Troll gizzard shad hooked through the nostrils to locate groups of stripers and maintain excellent depth control. Drifting with the wind over structural elements presents baits as silently as possible—essential when stripers are skittish.

Flatlines— Use flatlines or freelines to search for stripers holding near the surface or to pull active stripers from the depths. Flatlines consist of no weight or a single lead shot set about a foot above a single hook. Hook your biggest baits on flatlines to let the shad call stripers to them. Flatlines run within a few feet of the surface at 2 mph, but can be dropped to fish holding deeper by slowing the boat.

Trolling Livebait

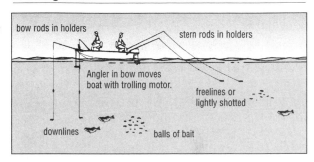

Downrigging

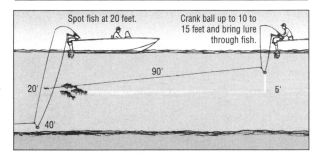

Balloons— Tying a partially inflated balloon around the line works like an oversized float, keeping baits away from the boat at a specific depth. They're inexpensive, offer adjustable buoyancy and position on the line, and are easy to see. Rig balloons on baits trolled near the surface, otherwise hooks are hard to set. Other rigs present baits more effectively in deeper water.

Downriggers— Downriggers are unbeatable for stripers suspending deeper than 30 feet. Use cannonballs from 8 to 12 pounds, and set lures from 50 to over 100 feet behind the cannonball for wary stripers. Set downriggers at the depth stripers predominately seem to be holding. Adjust the depth of the weight when you see fish on your electronics. □

Finding Striped Bass In Winter

S TARTING IN LATE FALL, COOLING water stimulates striped bass to begin feeding heavily. Alone or in schools, they attack baitfish from the surface down to the bottom. These big aggressive fish are within a day's drive of more than 50 million Americans, but they go almost unnoticed during winter. Bring your bass-casting arm and your pike lures, and get set for some of the hottest open-water action of the year.

Winter Hot Spots

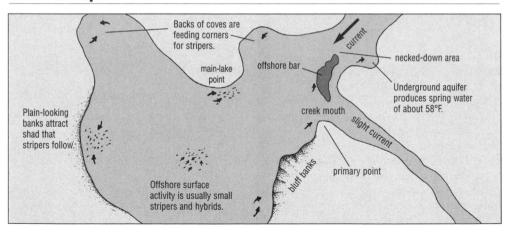

Backs of coves are feeding corners for stripers.

current

necked-down area

main-lake point

offshore bar

Underground aquifer produces spring water of about 58°F.

creek mouth

slight current

Plain-looking banks attract shad that stripers follow.

bluff banks

primary point

Offshore surface activity is usually small stripers and hybrids.

When—

Tackle— *Rod:* 6½- to 7½-foot heavy-power casting rod. *Reel:* large-capacity baitcasting reel. *Line:* 14- to 30-pound-test mono.

Rigging— Livebait catches stripers throughout winter, but lures allow for covering more water and exploring several depth options. Stripers force shad and other baitfish to the surface where the baitfish schools scatter, leaving disoriented individuals vulnerable. Topwater baits are effective, but baits that fall or glide like a crippled baitfish work, too. Spinners, spoons, jigs, and crankbaits also work well, while heavier spoons and jigs probe extreme depths. When fish are focused on 2½- to 5-inch threadfin shad, bass-size baits may outproduce those designed for stripers. Be sure to upgrade hooks and split-rings on these lures.

Location— The vertical position of stripers during summer is determined by water temperature and the oxygen content of water. Fall turnover frees fish to move vertically and horizontally, and stripers often occupy similar spots in all types of waters.

Dead-end coves—Groups of stripers push schools of shad into areas where the baitfish are confined on three sides. Shallow cover restricts escape and may be the scene of striper activity.

Bluffs—Stripers also suspend along bluff banks where the river channel runs close to a steep bank. Shad schools move along the channel edge in winter, often in deep water where the water's warmer.

Main-lake points—Timbered points often are resting areas for inactive stripers. Shad may winter along steep downstream sides and stripers may hold and feed there, too.

Springs—In many parts of the country, aquifers close to the surface produce flowing springs. Water ranges from 55°F to 58°F, depending on geological area. They're worth checking.

Necked-down areas—Where an impoundment narrows, usually offers more current and deeper water to attract stripers. Baitfish moving upstream or downstream must pass through this area. □

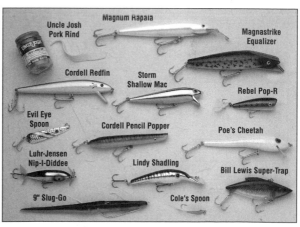

Leadline Trolling For Wipers

THE TENDENCY OF HYBRID STRIPED bass to suspend is a problem for most anglers because many hybrid fishermen were black bass fishermen first. Largemouth rarely suspend, and when they do, they're tough to catch. To catch suspended hybrids, these anglers typically drift over or anchor on a spot and present baits vertically. While these methods work, they're often not the most efficient way to put numbers of fish in the boat. Leadline trolling is efficient and will work wherever hybrids are found.

When—

Tackle—
Rods: 6½- to 7½-foot medium-power casting rod with a soft tip section. *Reel:* large-capacity baitcasting reel. *Line:* 18-pound-test leadcore main line and a 12-foot 10-pound-test mono leader.

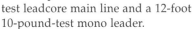

Rigging— Leadcore line is lead wire surrounded by dacron line. It comes in 100-yard spools and each 10-yard segment is marked with a different color. The size and weight of lures has little affect on running depth because the weight of the lead is dominant over the buoyancy or diving tendencies of lures. At slow speeds, lures can be trolled as deep as 50 feet, but the practical limit to leadcore is between 10 and 40 feet. If fish are closer to the surface,

Leadcore and light leaders cause lures to break off easily, so bring a few dozen of your favorite crankbaits, spoons, and spinners for fishing timbered impoundments.

mono works better; if they're deeper, down-riggers are more efficient.

Location—Once water temperatures rise into the 50°F range in spring, hybrid stripers typically gather around the mouths of tributaries, staging before their spawning run. Although hybrids are sterile, they retain the urge to migrate upstream to spawn. Before they head upstream, however, they're vulnerable to leadline trolling. In reservoirs without running tributaries, hybrids mill around in the mouths of bays and off points, often suspending 15 to 30 feet down over water 50 or more feet deep. After their false spawn, most hybrids return to the lower ends of reservoirs and form groups off points, over creek channels, or along bluffs.

Distinct structural elements often continue to produce fish through late fall.

Presentation—Using a foot-controlled bow-mount trolling motor to follow depth contours leaves both hands free to set rods, adjust lines, and fight fish. For two anglers each using a pair of rods, position the two forward rod holders perpendicular and parallel to the water. The rear rod holders should point straight back at a slight upward angle. This configuration allows different baits to be set at different depths without snagging. Once lines are set, the bow man guides the boat through known concentrations of fish. Or he makes S-turns across contours while watching for fish on sonar. Leadcore lines track well and rarely tangle, even on tight turns. □

Leadcore System

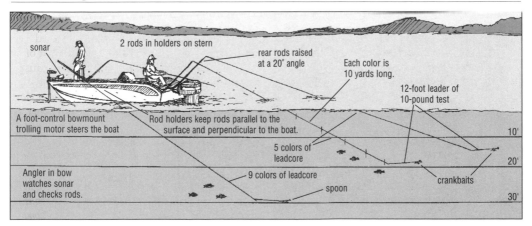

A foot-control bowmount trolling motor steers the boat

sonar

2 rods in holders on stern

rear rods raised at a 20° angle

Each color is 10 yards long.

12-foot leader of 10-pound test

Rod holders keep rods parallel to the surface and perpendicular to the boat.

5 colors of leadcore

Angler in bow watches sonar and checks rods.

9 colors of leadcore

spoon

crankbaits

10'

20'

30'

Tailrace Tactics For Hybrid Stripers

HYBRID STRIPED BASS ARE STOCKED into reservoirs across the southern two-thirds of the United States. They grow fast on threadfin shad. By their second or third spring, they weigh 3 to 5 pounds and are ready to migrate upstream. A hybrid genetic mix keeps them from reproducing, but their urge to ascend rivers to spawn is as strong as the urge in their parental species, the white and striped bass. Spawning fish may travel hundreds of miles upstream, but on most major rivers they soon are stopped by dams. A combination of big fish and fast water provides some of the most exciting fishing of the season.

Anatomy Of A Tailrace

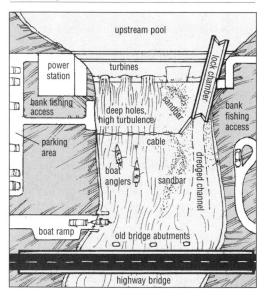

When—

A combination of factors key the spawning run.

The water temperature that triggers the initial migration and determines the duration of the journey is a mystery. But water temperatures in the upper 50°F range usually coincide with the arrival of large numbers of fish in tailraces. High flows caused by rain and runoff also attract large runs of hybrids. In Florida, at the southern end of the hybrid's range, they move into tailraces in February. The migration is initiated progressively later farther north. Wipers may not migrate until June in Illinois.

Tackle—*Rod:* 7- to 12-foot medium-heavy-power casting or spinning rod. *Reel:* large capacity baitcasting or spinning reel. *Line:* 12- to 17-pound-test abrasion-resistant mono.

Rigging—One- to 2-ounce jigs and spoons are the best lures for bank fishing. White bucktails with long twister tails or pork strips are most popular. If the bottom has boulders or rock crevices, choose wide stand-up heads to minimize snags.

Location—Stream fishermen look for boils, slicks, and eddies, which indicate fish-holding structure. But in a tailrace, the river reacts more to man-made influences than to natural laws. Conflicting flows move sand, gravel, and even chunk-rock, forming humps and bars. Hybrids often congregate upstream of humps because they slow current and let fish move and feed more efficiently. Wing dams and lock-chamber walls break flow and create sand flats downstream. Hybrids roam and feed here if the water level is high, but usually only white bass and suckers will be on flats less than 8 feet deep.

Presentation—Cast upstream of a structural element, current break, or backflow edge. Let the lure sink as it washes downstream toward the target. Maintain feel because strikes may come as the lure drifts. Work it through a

Hybrid Lure Selection

Key Current Breaks

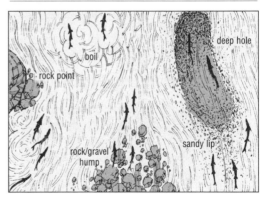

portion of the break and then reel in. Use a series of casts to probe each portion of a current break. Hybrids often strike lures from a particular angle. Fish jigs and spoons with an exaggerated lift-drop retrieve. □

Ice-Fishing For White Bass

WHITE BASS PROVIDE SOME OF WINTER'S fastest fishing, but only after a school is located. Finding them, however, isn't easy. Their location and behavior in a body of water depend on type of lake or reservoir, available forage, and population size. Where large populations exists, whites often seem to be everywhere—on bars, along bars, in open water, deep, and shallow. But white bass are not structure-oriented and often roam, looking for food. Even when you catch a few fish in a general area, don't expect them to stay in specific spots for long. To consistently find these efficient predators under the ice, it's necessary to hit high-percentage spots, drill holes, and fish fast until you contact fish.

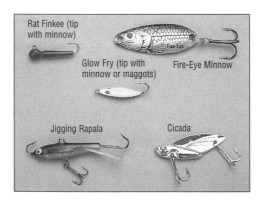

Rat Finkee (tip with minnow)

Glow Fry (tip with minnow or maggots)

Fire-Eye Minnow

Jigging Rapala

Cicada

When—

Tackle— *Rod:* 2- to 3-foot light-power ice rod. *Reel:* small-capacity spinning reel. *Line:* 4- to 8-pound-test mono.

Rigging— Generally choose larger lures that fish more aggressively than typical panfish lures. Try flash lures like 1/4-ounce jigging spoons; swimming lures like #3, #5, or #7

Jigging Rapalas; or 1/8-ounce leadhead jigs tipped with maggots or minnows.

Location—High-percentage spots for white bass and crappies are similar. Check obvious structural elements like points and other areas that tend to congregate baitfish. Also, check current areas and necked-down areas. Causeways and narrow channels are another possibility. A causeway, long point, or inside turn in the shoreline drop-off attracts and holds more baitfish and white bass than open water areas do.

During early ice, whites also tend to be in shallower water than later in the season. Even during midwinter, though, they rarely stay for long deeper than forty feet. In reservoirs and natural lakes, white bass move through open water until gathered by a structural element that sticks into the lake basin. If they find forage as they move around the element, they often stay until the forage is thinned.

Presentation—Use an aggressive jigging presentation most of the time, since white

bass often compete aggressively for food. Catching them is usually a matter of getting the fish to see the bait. When white bass seem less aggressive, try smaller swim and flash lures worked less aggressively. Rarely, however, will you need to resort to small ice flies or other subtle presentations. □

Productive Locations

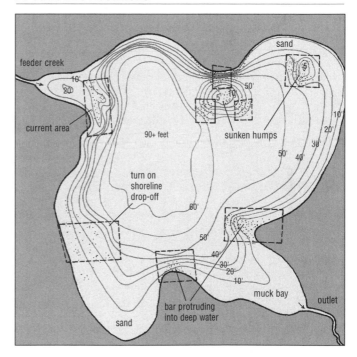

feeder creek
sand
current area
90+ feet
sunken humps
turn on shoreline drop-off
bar protruding into deep water
muck bay
outlet
sand

White Bass Location In Reservoirs

WHITE BASS ARE NATIVE TO THE Great Lakes and the Mississippi River system, but the creation of reservoirs on major rivers across most of the United States has greatly expanded their range. Like their larger cousins the striped bass, packs of hungry white bass push schools of shad to the surface. Anglers who locate these surface-feeding whites experience some of the most exciting fishing in freshwater. Unlike crappies and bluegill, however, white bass often hold in open water, far from cover. Catching them when they're not boiling on the surface requires an understanding of their seasonal and daily movements.

When—

Tackle— *Rod:* 6- to 7-foot light-power spinning rod. *Reel:* medium-capacity spinning reel with a long-cast spool. *Line:* 6- or 8-pound-test mono. □

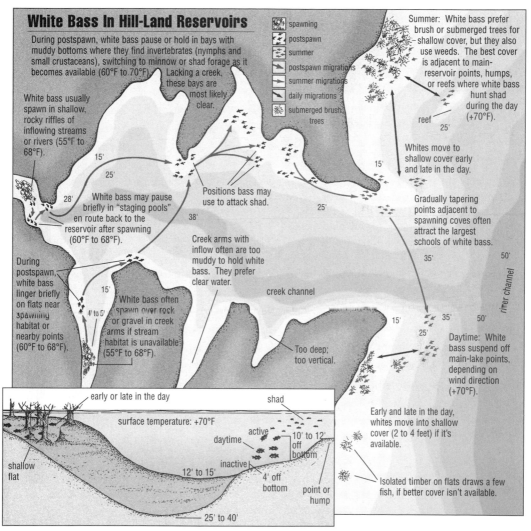

White Bass In Hill-Land Reservoirs

During postspawn, white bass pause or hold in bays with muddy bottoms where they find invertebrates (nymphs and small crustaceans), switching to minnow or shad forage as it becomes available (60°F to 70°F). Lacking a creek, these bays are most likely clear.

White bass usually spawn in shallow, rocky riffles of inflowing streams or rivers (55°F to 68°F).

White bass may pause briefly in "staging pools" en route back to the reservoir after spawning (60°F to 68°F).

During postspawn, white bass linger briefly on flats near spawning habitat or nearby points (60°F to 68°F).

White bass often spawn over rock or gravel in creek arms if stream habitat is unavailable (55°F to 68°F).

Positions bass may use to attack shad.

Creek arms with inflow often are too muddy to hold white bass. They prefer clear water.

creek channel

Too deep; too vertical.

Summer: White bass prefer brush or submerged trees for shallow cover, but they also use weeds. The best cover is adjacent to main-reservoir points, humps, or reefs where white bass hunt shad during the day (+70°F).

reef

Whites move to shallow cover early and late in the day.

Gradually tapering points adjacent to spawning coves often attract the largest schools of white bass.

river channel

Daytime: White bass suspend off main-lake points, depending on wind direction (+70°F).

Early and late in the day, whites move into shallow cover (2 to 4 feet) if it's available.

Isolated timber on flats draws a few fish, if better cover isn't available.

Legend:
- spawning
- postspawn
- summer
- postspawn migrations
- summer migrations
- daily migrations
- submerged brush trees

15' 25' 28' 38' 15' 4' to 5' 15' 25' 35' 50' 35' 50' 25' 15'

early or late in the day

shad

surface temperature: +70°F

active

daytime

10' to 12' off bottom

inactive

shallow flat

12' to 15'

4' off bottom

point or hump

25' to 40'

White Perch In Tidal Rivers

CLOSE RELATIVES TO THE STRIPED bass, white perch originally occurred in waters along the Atlantic Coast from Nova Scotia to South Carolina. This species tolerates a range of salinities, from pure freshwater to nearly 100 percent saltwater, so it thrives in tidal rivers. Its tolerance of freshwater, ability to quickly expand its population, and opportunistic feeding habits have allowed it to move far inland during the last 50 years. Many large perch are now caught in inland lakes and reservoirs, but the biggest whites—those weighing one to two or more pounds—are still taken from tidal rivers.

Joe Tomelleri

When—

Tackle— *Rod:* 6½- to 12-foot medium-heavy-power spinning or casting rod. *Reel:* medium-capacity spinning or baitcasting reel. *Line:* 10- to 15-pound-test abrasion-resistant mono.

Rigging—Tackle for white perch in brackish water is more stout than the gear used in lakes and reservoirs. During a strong tide, 1- to 3-ounce sinkers are needed to hold baits in current.

Snap a pyramid sinker onto a snap-swivel so it slides above a barrel swivel, 2-foot leader, and hook. Sea-run white perch eat sandworms, bloodworms, shrimp, killies or other baitfish, and small crabs. They all make fine baits, though bloodworms are most available in bait shops.

Location—White perch spawn in April and May in southern New England, running upstream from the lower portions of estuaries to gravel shoals and emergent grasses where females lay batches of small sticky eggs. Unlike their close relatives the striped and white bass, white perch may spawn over a period of several weeks. And unlike many anadromous species, white perch feed heavily during their spawning run.

The incoming tide often sparks the highest white perch activity. Plan to be on the water a couple of hours before high tide and continue fishing until the tide begins to turn. When the run is hot, however, good fishing may continue into an outgoing tide. Outside bends in the river and the mouths of ditches or feeder creeks are top spots.

After the spawn, white perch return to the lower estuary or into large bays to feed. Chesapeake Bay holds vast numbers of perch that spawn in dozens of tributaries in Delaware, Maryland, and Pennsylvania. Similar fishing opportunities exist before, during, and after the spawning run in tidal rivers and estuaries across much of the Atlantic Coast. Boat fishing and wading are both productive, but few anglers target perch, due to the many other fishing options available. ☐

Basic Slip Rig

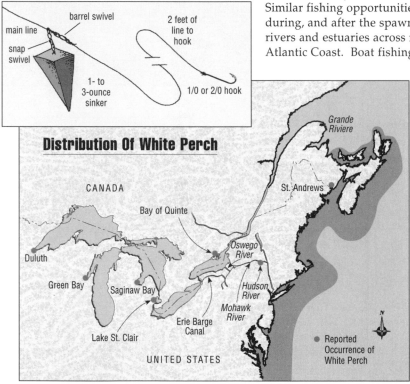

main line
barrel swivel
snap swivel
1- to 3-ounce sinker
2 feet of line to hook
1/0 or 2/0 hook

Distribution Of White Perch

CANADA

Grande Riviere

St. Andrews

Bay of Quinte

Oswego River

Duluth

Green Bay

Saginaw Bay

Hudson River

Mohawk River

Lake St. Clair

Erie Barge Canal

UNITED STATES

● Reported Occurrence of White Perch

Fishing For Sturgeon

M OST OF THE WORLD'S 25 species of sturgeon inhabit central and eastern Europe. Recreational fisheries exist for three species in North America— the lake, green, and white sturgeon. Shovelnose sturgeon may be taken in some areas, but their small size, feeding habits, and habitat preferences render them only incidentally catchable. The most popular sturgeon fishery occurs on the Columbia River. Anglers there spend more time pursuing white sturgeon than salmon, steelhead, or giant walleyes. Modifications of their basic tactics will work for whites or other species of sturgeon in rivers of all sizes.

Typical Sturgeon Rig

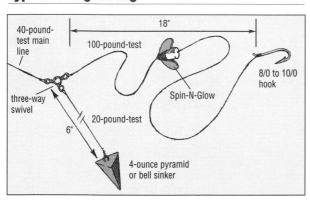

40-pound-test main line

100-pound-test

18"

Spin-N-Glow

8/0 to 10/0 hook

three-way swivel

20-pound-test

6"

4-ounce pyramid or bell sinker

When— Variables like time of year, water temperature, and dam generation schedules all affect the activity level of the fish. Sturgeon generally favor baits abundant in the river, feeding most actively when dead fish are passing through the turbines of hydroelectric dams. Peak feeding takes place when water temperature is between 50 °F and 65 °F. Large sturgeon seem to feed little when the water is cooler than 42 °F and also are less active in water over 65 °F, though small fish may bite any time.

October, November, May, and June usually are considered the best months to tackle trophy white sturgeon across most of their range.

Tackle— *Rod:* 5½- to 11-foot heavy-power casting rods. *Reel:* large-capacity baitcasting reel with a free-spool clicker. *Line:* 40- to 80-pound-test braided or abrasion-resistant mono line.

Rigging— The white sturgeon is the largest and perhaps most powerful freshwater fish in North America, and will quickly exploit any weakness in your terminal tackle. The most popular rig consists of a three-way swivel with a 6-inch dropper line on one loop holding the sinker. Sinker weight depends on depth and current velocity, as well as the style of sinker. Pyramid or bell sinkers, for example, rather than egg sinkers, hold better on the broken-rock bottoms sturgeon favor. The leader is an 18-inch length of heavy mono tied to an 8/0 to 10/0 hook. Attractors like Spin-N-Glows or Corkies often are added to the leader above the hook. □

Dam Strategy

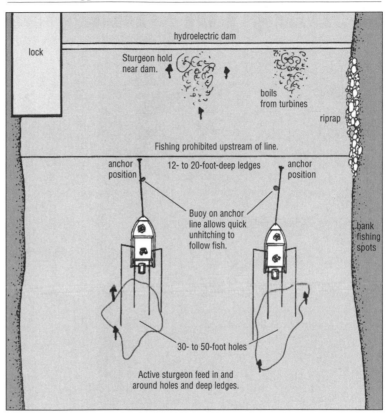

lock

hydroelectric dam

Sturgeon hold near dam.

boils from turbines

riprap

Fishing prohibited upstream of line.

anchor position

12- to 20-foot-deep ledges

anchor position

Buoy on anchor line allows quick unhitching to follow fish.

bank fishing spots

30- to 50-foot holes

Active sturgeon feed in and around holes and deep ledges.

Fishing For American Shad

When—Each spring, shad run up Atlantic coast rivers from Newfoundland to the St. Johns in Florida, with time of migration linked to water temperature. In the St. Johns, the migration may peak in mid-January when water temperature is in the mid-50°F range, and occurring progressively later northward, with runs as late as July, north of the St. Lawrence River.

I F THE WORD SHAD CONJURES IMAGES of an oily baitfish whose only mission in life is to bolster the growth rates of bass, walleyes, stripers, and other sportfish, think again. Historical evidence suggests that huge schools of migrating American shad fed George Washington's starving troops during the winter of 1777 and 1778. Today, runs of anadromous American shad continue to sustain many popular sportfisheries. Shad fishing is spectacular fun—these fish possess the characteristic pulling power of migratory saltwater fish. Add their leaping ability and broad sides, which they use to advantage in current, and you have all you can handle on medium-weight spinning equipment.

Tackle— *Rod:* 6- to 7-foot light-power spinning rod. *Reel:* medium-capacity spinning reel. *Line:* 4- or 6-pound-test mono.

Rigging— Although shad don't feed once they enter freshwater, they instinctively bite small lures and flies. Angling for shad has been popular in northern rivers for decades and is growing fast in southern and western rivers. The most popular lures are shad darts—small leadhead jigs tied with sparse bucktail. Some theoreticians claim that darts resemble the small shrimp that shad eat in the ocean, but spinners, small spoons, streamers, and other styles of jigs are effective as well.

Presentation— In rivers, shad follow current seams between fast and slack water. Quartering casts across current is most effective. Retrieve baits steadily for the best hookup percentage. Large groups of shad also hold behind islands, points, jetties, or other current breaks, seemingly resting during their journey. Areas like dams that prevent or constrict migration also are high-percentage areas.

Restoration— The primary factor for angling success is the abundance of shad. Shad runs are well synchronized and massive

Distribution Of American Shad

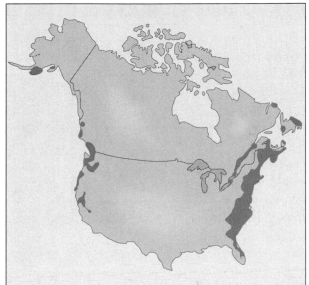

on some rivers. Since runs on the Hudson River have been revitalized, gillnetters harvest about 350,000 pounds per year. On the Connecticut River, restoration efforts have brought more than half a million shad back each year, where they're primarily caught throughout New England. On the Columbia River, recent runs are estimated at around 4 million fish, apparently enough for tribal fishermen, commercial netters, and recreational anglers. □

In Pursuit Of Paddlefish

WHAT NORTH American fish can grow to over 100 pounds, has no teeth, eats microscopic plankton, and resembles a shark with a big nose? If you solved this riddle, you're familiar with the paddlefish, one of our largest, oldest, and most fascinating fish. In early America, paddlefish inhabited the large free-flowing rivers of the Mississippi Valley, extending north into Ontario and west to the Missouri River in Montana. Dam construction later eliminated theses fish from several river drainages and several states. Today, they also thrive in some impoundments, and remain in 22 states.

Snagging Rig

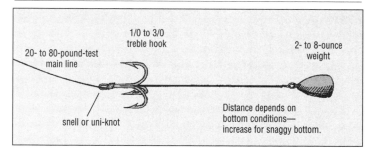

20- to 80-pound-test main line

snell or uni-knot

1/0 to 3/0 treble hook

2- to 8-ounce weight

Distance depends on bottom conditions— increase for snaggy bottom.

Rigging— Paddlefish feed by swimming through clouds of zooplankton and engulfing the tiny organisms that can't swim out of their way. Their long thin gill rakers strain the water and filter out the plankton. Since they rarely take bait or lures, anglers catch them with weighted snagging hooks—jerked in the hope they will contact a fish. This method works particularly well when paddlefish migrate upstream in spring and congregate below dams.

Conservation—Several states have begun stocking programs to maintain populations of this unique fish, but regulations allow limited harvest in conjunction with the traditional popularity of snagging. In Kansas, Montana, and North Dakota, snaggers may obtain two tags per season, which they must attach to paddlefish as hunters tag deer. All fish snagged must be kept to prevent the release of wounded fish and to ensure that the harvest includes juveniles as well as adults.

Because of the grave problem of poachers slaughtering paddlefish for their roe, which is used to make caviar, the sale or barter of paddlefish is illegal. The value of the roe, which can exceed $20 per pound for processed eggs, has spurred the development of commercial aquaculture for paddlefish. Despite restrictions on snagging, however, substantial harvest continues across much of the paddlefish's range.

Where natural spawning areas for paddlefish remain, it's critical that channelization or damming be prohibited and that pollution be minimized. Harvest must be carefully monitored to ensure that populations aren't reduced to a point at which spawning is limited. In populations sustained by stocking, harvest should be limited to allow these ancient, magnificent fish to maintain their presence in our rivers. □

Distribution Of Paddlefish

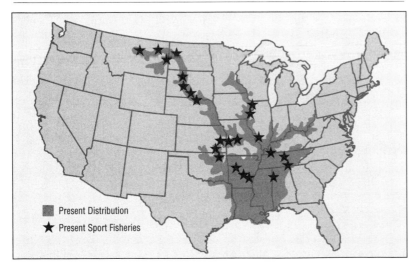

Present Distribution
★ Present Sport Fisheries

Rigs And Tactics For Gar

I T DOESN'T MATTER IF YOU'RE TALKING about 200-pound alligator gar in a Texas reservoir, a 3-foot longnose in a Minnesota river, or a 5-pound shortnose in an Arkansas slough—they're all first-class sportfish. They're all willing biters, too, often revealing their location during summer by rolling on the surface to gulp air. They're also powerful fighters who will launch their muscular armor-plated body into the air when hooked. The problem with gar is their tooth-filled mouth and habit of running long distances with a bait before swallowing it. This makes them difficult to hook and land with traditional rigs. But a handful of modified rigs will catch any species of gar wherever they swim.

Hooks—Gar lack any appreciable amount of flesh in their mouth, making hookups with

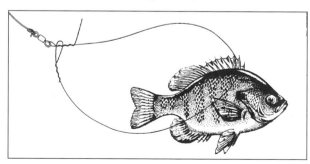

large single hooks difficult. Small sharp treble hooks penetrate faster and the additional hook points increase your chance of a good set. Lip hook a baitfish with a #6 to #2 treble hook on a set or float rig. Gar often grab the bait sideways and slowly swim off. Wait until the fish stops and starts to swallow the bait. When he starts to run again, set the hook firmly. Quick-strike rigs and lures with multiple treble hooks increase your chance of a hookup without risking injury caused by swallowed hooks.

Snares—Wire snares like those used to catch rabbits may be the most effective gar rig of all. Make a snare by wrapping one end of a 2-foot piece of stainless steel wire around a heavy barrel swivel. Run the free end of the wire through the back of a lively baitfish, just below the dorsal fin. Swing the free end back toward the swivel and form a loose loop that slides easily on the leader. Tie your main line to the swivel and cast the rig onto a shallow flat. When a gar grabs the bait, a firm pull will tighten the snare around its beak.

Ropes— Versatile lures and flies also can be fashioned from strands of frayed nylon rope. Cut a 3- to 6-inch piece of 3/8-inch nylon rope, and thread it onto the shank of a hook, jighead, or spinnerbait as you would a plastic worm. Use a flame to fuse the rope to the hook shank, then wrap over the melted rope with strong thread or braided line. Cover the thread wraps with a couple coats of epoxy to increase the lure's durability. Unravel the nylon strands the the base of the head, and you're ready to fish. When a gar strikes, the lure becomes tangled in its teeth and around its snout.

Jugs— Jugs, or pop-ups as they're called in the south, are similar to the juglines used by catfishermen. They consist of a 4-foot section of PVC pipe or a sturdy branch tied to 2-liter soda bottle. One end of a 2-foot wire leader is attached to the branch, the other to a large study hook baited with livebait or cutbait.

Fleets of jugs are drifted across shallow flats at night. When a fish begins its second run, indicating it has swallowed the bait, the angler grabs the limb and attempts to haul the fish aboard. □

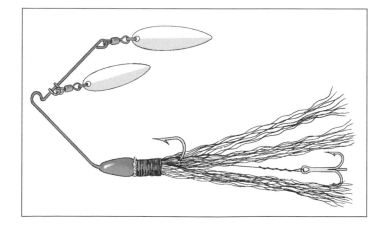

Ice-Fishing For Burbot

BURBOT IS ONE OF MANY COMMON names for *Lota lota*, the only freshwater member of the cod family. In most areas, anglers have overlooked the sporting and table qualities of this fish. Some anglers would rather cut their line than handle these slimy creatures that look like a cross between a snake and a bullhead. The truth is, however, that burbot are fun to catch, typically large, and make a fine meal when properly prepared.

When—

Tackle— *Rod:* 2- to 3-foot medium-power ice rod. *Reel:* small-capacity spinning reel. *Line:* 8- to 12-pound-test mono.

Rigging— Match the size and action of your lure to the activity level of the fish.

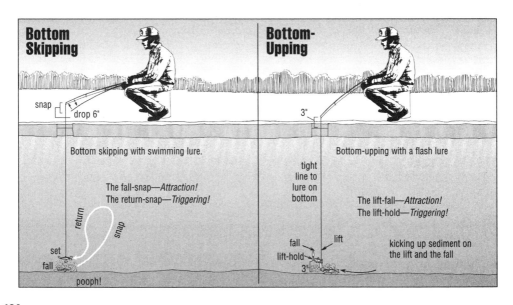

Bottom Skipping

snap

drop 6"

Bottom skipping with swimming lure.

The fall-snap—*Attraction!*
The return-snap—*Triggering!*

return
snap

set
fall
pooph!

Bottom-Upping

3"

tight line to lure on bottom

Bottom-upping with a flash lure

The lift-fall—*Attraction!*
The lift-hold—*Triggering!*

fall   lift
lift-hold
3"

kicking up sediment on the lift and the fall

Generally, the same baits you would use for walleyes will work for burbot. Attract active fish with a swim bait like a #5 or #7 Jigging Rapala with a fish eye or minnow head impaled on the treble hook. For less active fish, anchor a lively 4-inch shiner or chub with a 1/3-ounce phosphorescent jigging spoon. Finally hook a 4-inch livebait on a 1/4-ounce plain leadhead jig for negative fish. Aggressive jigging attracts fish, but use subtle hops or twitches on or near the bottom to trigger interested burbot.

Location— Burbot inhabit northern lakes, rivers, and even brackish estuaries around the globe. They're common throughout most of Canada, Alaska, and the northern tier of states from Maine to eastern Washington. Despite this wide distribution, however, little is known about the movements of the species. We do know they prefer deep water for most of the year and that they spawn on shallow gravel bars from late January through March across much of their range. The best fishing occurs a few weeks before burbot spawn on bars and humps adjacent to deep water, as the fish gather to feed on small fish and crayfish.

Tight-Line Twitching

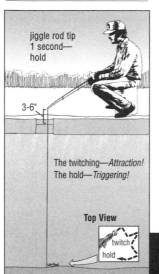

jiggle rod tip 1 second— hold

3-6"

The twitching—*Attraction!*
The hold—*Triggering!*

Top View

twitch
hold

Preparing— Fillet a burbot as you would a walleye, and remove the skin. The ribs are thick and easily removed, and the tail section has no bones beyond the spine. Burbot are rather oily, so parboil fillets for a couple minutes in a pot of simmering water with a tablespoon or two of lemon juice. Any of your favorite recipes will work, but it's tough to beat pan-fried burbot prepared right on the ice with fried potatoes and onions. □

All About Bowfin

THE NORTH AMERICAN BOWFIN IS A phylogenetic relict, the last survivor of a great family of related fishes *(Amiidae)* that thrived almost worldwide from about 200 to 50 million years ago. Seeing one is a bit like gawking at an old Model T rattling down main street. The large, ganoid scales, the flattened bony head, and the long rippling dorsal fin may appear ugly to some, but biologists nod approvingly. They just don't make 'em like that anymore.

When—

Tackle— *Rod:* 6- to 7-foot medium-heavy-power casting or spinning rod. *Reel:* medium-capacity baitcasting or spinning reel. *Line:* 12- to 17-pound-test mono.

Rigging— Most bowfin catches are accidental. They sometimes attack bass lures, but not consistently. If you catch one on a spinnerbait, you could spend weeks throwing spinnerbaits to visible bowfin without a follow. The best rigs for bowfin are similar to those for catfish—float and set rigs baited with livebait or cutbait. The paternoster rig is particularly effective, as it allows an anchored baitfish to swim around above the bottom to attract bowfin.

Location— The preferred habitat of bowfin in the south is swampy weedy bays in lakes, rivers, or backwaters. In the north, they thrive in similar eutrophic habitat, and most spend the summer in shallow weedy bays. During late summer and early fall, they usually head for deeper weedlines in main basins and deep bays. In winter, they're typically in 15- to 30-foot depths.

Bowfin are spring spawners, making nests near shore in substrate similar to what largemouth bass use, though they can tolerate a muckier bottom. Optimum water temperatures are 60°F to 66°F. Nests are typically 1 to 2 feet deep and 15 to 24 inches in diameter. The male rigorously defends the nest and is likely to attack any large bait or lure that ventures too close.

Presentation— Bowfin have few devoted fans, but their savage strikes and determined battles mark them as a first-class sportfish. If you're on a lake with a known plenitude of bowfin, consider tossing a chunk of cutbait into a shallow bay. Use a float rig over soft bottom areas. Bowfin often come off bottom to feed, as evidenced by their infrequent attacks on topwater lures. But if bait—live or dead—offers a diminished possibility of escape, bowfin approach in a chewing mode. □

Paternoster Rig

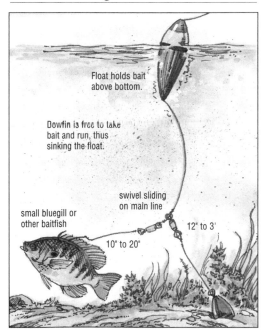

Float holds bait above bottom.

Dowfin is free to take bait and run, thus sinking the float.

swivel sliding on main line

small bluegill or other baitfish

10" to 20"

12" to 3'

Catching And Preparing American Eels

I N NORTH AMERICA AND PERHAPS BEYOND, the American eel is the obvious winner in the strange and mysterious freshwater fish categories. They more closely resemble a snake in appearance and locomotion, but are as much a fish as bass and walleyes. Of course bass don't wrap their bodies around your arm while you try to unhook them and walleyes don't crawl across damp fields in search of worms. But eels are familiar to those who fish for catfish, carp, and other sportfish—they're catchable with well-presented natural baits, put up a memorable struggle, and are the basis of a fine meal when properly prepared.

When—

Tackle— *Rod:* 6- to 11-foot medium-power spinning rod. *Reel:* medium-capacity spinning reel. *Line:* 6- to 10-pound-test abrasion-resistant mono.

Rigging— Eels are opportunistic feeders, eating insect larvae, small minnows, dead fish, and anything else they can catch or find on the bottom. Their sense of taste is more acute than the channel cat's, so few edible organisms go unnoticed. Night crawlers, small pieces of oily cutbait, and chicken livers are proven eel attractors. The same slip and drift rigs used for catfish catch eels. Use #6 to #2 long-shank hooks to match their small mouths, but don't use light-wire models—even small eels pull hard enough to quickly straighten an Aberdeen-style hook.

Location—

American eel are catadromous, meaning they spawn in the ocean, but live most of their lives in freshwater. In the spring, eels migrate from ponds and headwater streams to the open ocean. Precisely where they spawn remains a mystery, but their one-way journey is thousands of miles long. Young eels then drift in the Gulf Stream for a year before arriving at the North American coast. Male eels remain in brackish water estuaries, but females may move hundreds of miles inland. They move overland around barriers like dams until they reach suitable ponds and streams. They hold in deep, quiet water during the day and emerge at night to feed.

Distribution Of American Eel

Presentation—
Fishing for eels is not unlike fishing for bullheads, except eels are even harder to hold once caught. In ponds, lakes, and sloughs, cast bait rigs to shallow flats adjacent to deep water. In rivers, look for riffles at the head of a deep hole or quiet backwater areas near deep water. Dams concentrate migrating eels by temporarily blocking their upstream migration and distracting them with a steady supply of dead or injured baitfish. They often nibble gently at a bait, but quickly swallow the hook if you don't set immediately. To handle an eel you want to keep or release, dip your hand in water then press your palm into dry sand—this improves your grip on their slick skin.

Preparation—
Skin an eel by wrapping a stout cord around its neck just behind the gills. Cut a ring through the skin just below the cord, being careful not to cut too deeply into the flesh. Grasp the skin with a pliers and peel it off all the way down to the tail. Remove the head, fins, and entrails, and it's ready for baking, frying, or smoking. ☐

Fishing For Freshwater Drum

H OW IS THE VALUE OF A GAMEFISH MEASURED? If accessibility, fighting ability, and palatability deserve any merit, the freshwater drum must rank near the top of the list. How accessible? Drum have the largest latitudinal range of any freshwater fish in North America—from the Nelson River in Manitoba to the Rio Usumacinto system in Guatemala, a span of over 2,500 miles. How sporting? They readily take natural and artificial baits and fight harder than largemouth bass. How tasty? Some prefer the drum's firm, white, and boneless fillets to walleye.

When—

Tackle— *Rod:* 6½- to 7½-foot medium- or medium-heavy-power spinning or casting rod. *Reel:* medium-capacity spinning or baitcasting reel. *Line:* 10- to 20- pound-test mono.

Rigging— Natural baits and artificial lures presented on the bottom are most effective. Drum

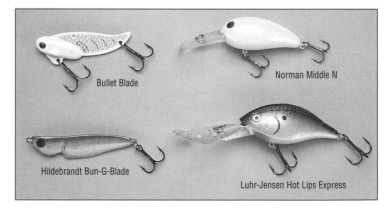

Bullet Blade

Norman Middle N

Hildebrandt Bun-G-Blade

Luhr-Jensen Hot Lips Express

feed primarily on insect larvae, crayfish, clams, and other organisms that live on the bottom of lakes and rivers, and therefore are accustomed to foraging down. Drifting float rigs or swimming jigs a foot or two off the bottom often fails to trigger neutral fish. Natural baits like crayfish tails, night crawlers, and cutbait will catch drum, but artificials trigger more strikes when fish are active. Deep-diving crankbaits, jigging spoons, bladebaits, and other lures scuffed along the bottom are most effective.

Location— The drum's widespread distribution is due in part to its sophisticated sensory system. Large earbones enhance hearing and allow for orienting in dark or turbid water. The long lateral line, which extends from the gill to the tip of the tail, also increases the fish's ability to locate and attack prey where vision is limited. So while drum prefer clear water, they're obviously equipped to thrive in adverse conditions. In rivers, drum prefer a hard bottom with moderate current—the edge of flats and the base of riprap shorelines are ideal locations. In lakes, they prefer shallow flats with little weedgrowth.

Drum Distribution

Presentation— Cast bladebaits upstream of your target to allow it to reach bottom. Reel in slack line as you raise your rod tip to a 30-degree angle. Slowly raise your rod to 45 degrees so the lure almost drags across the bottom, then move your rod tip back down as you retrieve slack line. Dig crankbaits down to the bottom, then adjust your retrieve speed to maintain contact. Set rigs are easier for drum to locate in fast or murky water, but drift rigs cover more water in moderate current. □

Where And How To Catch Whitefish

L AKE WHITEFISH INHABIT large infertile lakes and river systems in the northern tier of the United States, all of Alaska, and across Canada, from the the Atlantic to the Pacific coast. Despite the short growing season and harsh environment, whitefish often grow large—one taken off Isle Royale around 1918 weighed an incredible 42 pounds. Today, lake whitefish rarely exceed 15 pounds, but fish from 4 to 8 pounds are common. These fish readily attack artificial lures, and once hooked, they pull like a smallmouth and jump like a baby tarpon. They're also abundant in some waters and always provide an excellent meal. You may

not book a whitefish-only fly-in trip after catching one, but you won't go into whitefish country without light tackle either.

When—

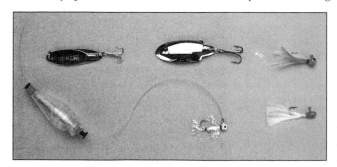

Tackle— *Rod:* 6- to 7½-foot light- to medium-power spinning rod. *Reel:* medium-capacity spinning reel. *Line:* 6- to 10-pound-test mono.

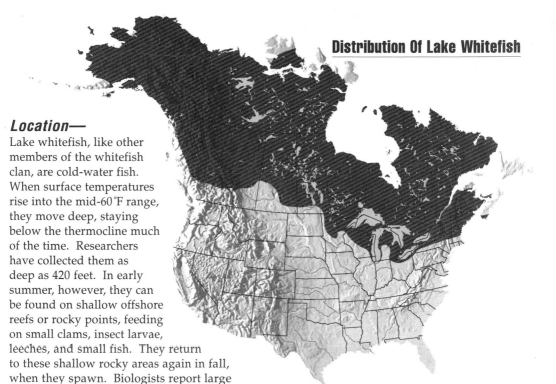

Distribution Of Lake Whitefish

Location—

Lake whitefish, like other members of the whitefish clan, are cold-water fish. When surface temperatures rise into the mid-60°F range, they move deep, staying below the thermocline much of the time. Researchers have collected them as deep as 420 feet. In early summer, however, they can be found on shallow offshore reefs or rocky points, feeding on small clams, insect larvae, leeches, and small fish. They return to these shallow rocky areas again in fall, when they spawn. Biologists report large spawning groups leaping over shallow reefs with water temperatures only in the upper 40°F range.

Presentation— It's hard to beat 1/16-ounce marabou jigs or small in-line spinners, but in lakes with large northern pike populations, expect to get bit off continually. A small jig suspended beneath a float or casting bubble near the surface still takes lots of whitefish, but won't attract as many pike. This rig can also be drifted or slowly retrieved across rocky reefs and points without hanging up. Just before dark, whitefish sipping emerging insects from the surface film often hit dry flies presented on a fly rod or casting bubble, or small compact spoons like Acme Kastmasters or Little Cleos. Trolling spoons also is effective later in the season when whitefish suspend over deep water. □

Glossary

Action: Measure of rod performance that describes the bend of a rod; ranges from slow to fast.

Anal Fin: Fin located on the ventral side of most fish, between the anal pore and tail.

Angler: Person using pole or rod and reel to catch fish.

Backwater: Shallow area off a river.

Baitfish: Small fish often eaten by predators.

Bar: Long ridge in a body of water. Sometimes called a shoal.

Bay: Major indentation in the shoreline of a lake or reservoir.

Bell Sinker: Pear-shaped sinker with brass eye on top.

Brackish: Water of intermediate salinity between seawater and freshwater.

Break: Distinct variation in otherwise constant stretches of cover, structure, or bottom type.

Breakline: Area of abrupt change in depth, bottom type, or water quality.

Cabbage: Any of several species of submerged weeds of the genus Potamogeton.

Canal: Man-made waterway for navigation.

Channel: The bed of a stream or river.

Coontail: Submerged aquatic plant of the hornwort family, typically found in hard water; characterized by stiff, forked leaves.

Cove: An indentation along the shoreline of a lake or reservoir.

Cover: Natural or man-made objects on the bottom of lakes, rivers, or impoundments, especially those that influence fish behavior.

Crankbait: Lipped diving lure.

Crustacean: Hard-shelled, typically aquatic invertebrate.

Current: Water moving in one direction, which may be interrupted or redirected over objects.

Dam: Man-made barrier to water flow.

Dark-Bottom Bay: Shallow, protected bay with a layer of dark organic material on the bottom that warms quickly in spring.

Diurnal: Occurring within a 24-hour daily period.

Dorsal Fin: Fin located on center of a fish's back.

Drag: System for allowing fish to pull line from reel while antireverse switch is engaged.

Drainage: The area drained by a river and all its tributaries.

Drop-Off: An area of substantial increase in depth.

Eddy: Area of slack water or reversed current in a stream or river.

Egg Sinker: Egg-shaped sinker with a hole from end to end.

Estuary: Area where a river meets saltwater and has characteristics of freshwater and marine environments.

Euro-Style: Similar to fishing tackle designed in Europe, especially floats, rods, and rigs.

Farm Pond: Small man-made body of water.

Feeder Creek: Tributary to a stream.

Feeding Strategy: Behaviors used for capture of prey.

Fingerling: Juvenile fish, usually from 1 to 3 inches long.

Fisherman: Person catching fish by any means, usually by angling.

Fishing Pressure: Amount of angling on a body of water in a period of time, usually measured in hours per acre per year; its effects on fish populations.

Flat: Area of lake, reservoir, or river characterized by little change in depth; may be shallow or deep.

Flippin': Presentation technique for dropping lures into dense cover at close range.

Flippin' Stick: Heavy-action fishing rod, 7 to 8 feet long, originally designed for bass fishing.

Float: Buoyant device for suspending bait.

Float Stop: Adjustable rubber bead or thread, set on line above float to determine fishing depth.

Fluorescent: Emits radiation when exposed to sunlight.

Forage: Something to be eaten; the act of eating.

Front: Weather system that causes changes in temperature, cloud cover, precipitation, wind, and barometric pressure.

Fry: Recently hatched fish.

Gamefish: Fish species pursued by anglers.

Gradient: Degree of slope in a stream or riverbed.

Habitat: Type of environment in which an organism usually lives.

Hole: Deep section of a stream or river.

Hybrid: Offspring of two species or subspecies.

Impoundment: Body of water formed by damming running water (a reservoir).

Invertebrate: Animal without a backbone.

Jig: Lure composed of lead-head with rigid hook, often with hair, plastic, rubber, or other dressings.

Jigworm: Plastic worm rigged on an open-hook jighead.

Lake: Confined area where water accumulates naturally.

Larva: Immature form of an organism.

Lateral Line: Sensory system of fish that detects low frequency vibrations in water.

Ledge: Sharp contour break in a river or reservoir.

Livebait: Any living animal used to entice fish to bite.

Location: Where fish position themselves in a body of water.

Migration: Directed movement by large number of animals of one species.

Minnowbait: Long, thin, minnow-shaped wood or plastic lure; a wobbling bait.

Monofilament: Fishing line made from a strand of synthetic fiber.

Nymph: Larval form of an insect.

Omnivore: Organism that eats a wide variety of items.

Open Water: The portion of a lake or reservoir away from flats and shoals.

Opportunistic: Feeding strategy in which items are eaten according to availability.

Overharvest: A level of fish harvest from a body of water that substantially reduces abundance of catchable fish, particularly large fish.

Oxbow: A U-shaped bend in a river.

Panfish: Group of about 30 small warm-water sportfish, including bullheads but not catfish.

Pattern: A defined set of location and presentation factors that consistently produce fish.

Pectoral Fin: Paired fin usually located on fish's side behind the head.

Pelagic: Living in open, off-shore waters.

Pelvic Fin: Paired fin usually located on lower body.

pH: A measure of hydrogen in concentration.

Phosphorescent: Ability to glow in the dark after exposure to a light source.

Pit: Area excavated for mining operations that fills with water.

Pitching: Presentation technique in which worms or jigs are dropped into cover at close range (15 to 30 feet) with an underhand, pendulum motion, using a 6- to 7-foot casting rod.

Plankton: Organisms drifting in a body of water.

Plug: Solid-bodied wood or plastic lure.

Point: Projection of land into a body of water.

Polarized: Capability of breaking up sunlight into directional components.

Pond: Small natural or man-made body of water.

Pool: Deep section of a stream or river.

Population: Group of animals of the same species within a geographical area that freely interbreed.

Postspawn: Period immediately after spawning; In-Fisherman calendar period between spawn and presummer.

Pound-Test: System for measuring the strength of fishing line; the amount of pressure that will break a line.

Predator: Fish that often feed on other fish.

Presentation: Combination of bait or lure, rig, tackle, and technique used to catch fish.

Prespawn: Period prior to spawning; In-Fisherman calendar period between winter and spawn.

Prey: Fish that often are eaten by other fish species.

Prop Bait: Topwater plug with one or more propellers at the front or back.

Quick-Strike Rig: European-style system for hooking live or dead baits, which includes 2 hooks and allows hooks to be set immediately following a strike.

Range: Area over which a species is distributed.

Rattlebait: Hollow-bodied, sinking, lipless crankbaits that rattle loudly due to shot and slugs in the body cavity.

Reeds: Any of several species of tall, leafless emergent aquatic weeds that grow in shallow zones of lakes and reservoirs.

Reef: Rocky hump in a body of water.

Reservoir: Large man-made body of water.

Resting Spot: Location used by fish not actively feeding.

Riffle: Shallow, fast-flowing section of a stream or river.

Rig: Arrangement of components for bait fishing, including hooks, leader, sinker, swivel, beads.

Riprap: Large rocks placed along a bank.

Riverine: Having characteristics of a river.

Run: Straight, moderate-depth section of a stream or river with little depth change.

Salinity: Concentration of salts in a liquid.

School: Group of fish of one species that move in unison.

Selective Harvest: Deciding to release or harvest fish, based on species, size, and relative abundance.

Sensory Organ: Biological system involved in sight, hearing, taste, smell, touch, or lateral line sense.

Set Rig: Rig that's cast into position on the bottom to await a strike.

Shot: Small, round sinkers pinched onto fishing line.

Silt: Fine sediment on the bottom of a body of water.

Sinkers: Variously shaped pieces of lead used to sink bait or lures.

Slip Float: Float with hole for sliding freely on line.

Slip Sinker: Sinker with a hole for sliding freely on line.

Slop: Dense aquatic vegetation matted on the surface.

Slough: Cove or backwater on a reservoir or river.

Slow Roll: Spinnerbait presentation in which the lure is retrieved slowly through and over cover objects.

Snag: Brush or tree in a stream or river.

Solitary: Occupying habitat without close association to other animals.

Sonar: Electronic fishing aid that emits sound waves underwater and interprets them to depict underwater objects.

Spawn: Reproduction of fish; In-Fisherman calendar period associated with that activity.

Species: Group of potentially interbreeding organisms.

Spine: Stiff, sharp segment of fin.

Spoon: Any of a variety of metal, plastic, or wood lures with a generally spoonlike shape and a single hook.

Sportfish: Fish species pursued by anglers.

Stock: Place fish in a body of water; population of animals.

Stress: State of physiological imbalance caused by disturbing environmental factors.

Strike: Biting motion of a fish.

Strike Window (Zone): Conceptual area in front of a fish within which it will strike food items or lures.

Structure: Changes in the shape of the bottom of lakes, rivers, or impoundments, especially those that influence fish behavior.

Stumpfield: Area of an impoundment where stands of timber have been cut prior to impoundment, leaving stumps below the surface.

Substrate: Type of bottom in a body of water.

Suspended Fish: Fish in open water hovering considerably above bottom.

Swim (Gas) Bladder: Organ of most bony fish that holds a volume of gas to make them neutrally buoyant at variable depths.

Tailwater: Area immediately downstream from a dam.

Temperature Tolerant: Able to function in a range of temperatures.

Terminal Tackle: Components of bait fishing system including hooks, sinkers, swivels, and leaders.

Thermocline: Layer of water with abrupt change in temperature, occurring between warm surface layer and cold bottom layer.

Topwaters: Lures designed to be worked on the surface.

Tracking: Following radio-tagged or sonic-tagged animals.

Trailer: A plastic skirt, grub, pork rind, livebait, or other attractor attached to a lure to entice fish.

Trailer Hook: An extra hook attached to a lure's rear hook to catch fish that strike behind the lure.

Transducer: Electronic part of a sonar unit that receives sound impulses and converts them to visual images.

Tributary: Stream or river flowing into a larger river.

Trigger: Characteristics of a lure or bait presentation that elicit a biting response in fish.

Trolling: Fishing method in which lures or baits are pulled by a boat.

Trolling Motor: Electric motor positioned on the bow or transom to push or pull the boat.

Turbid: Murky water, discolored by suspended sediment.

Turbulence: Water disturbed by strong currents.

Waterdog: Immature salamander possessing external gills.

Watershed: The region draining runoff into a body of water.

Weed: Aquatic plant.

Weedline (Weededge): Abrupt edge of a weedbed caused by a change in depth, bottom type, or other factor.

Wetland: Areas covered by water at least part of each year.

Wing Dam: Man-made earth or rock ridge to deflect current.

Winterkill: Fish mortality due to oxygen depletion under ice in late winter.

Year Class: Fish of one species hatched in a particular year.

Zooplankton: Tiny animals suspended in water.

Index